Texas Roots:
The Family of Vivian Childers
& Charles Cyrus

By Carla Whitacre Mayer

First Edition

2019
Family Memories Matter LLC
Wheaton, IL

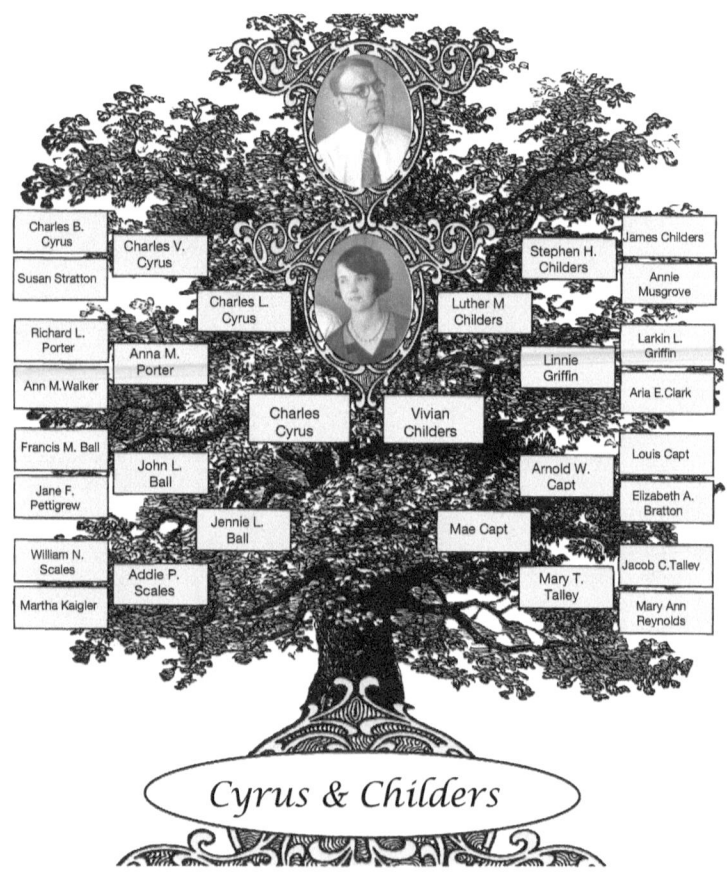

Charles B. Cyrus
Susan Stratton
Charles V. Cyrus
Charles L. Cyrus
Richard L. Porter
Anna M. Porter
Ann M. Walker
Charles Cyrus
Francis M. Ball
John L. Ball
Jane F. Pettigrew
Jennie L. Ball
William N. Scales
Addie P. Scales
Martha Kaigler

Stephen H. Childers
Luther M Childers
Vivian Childers
Arnold W. Capt
Mae Capt
Mary T. Talley

James Childers
Annie Musgrove
Larkin L. Griffin
Linnie Griffin
Aria E. Clark
Louis Capt
Elizabeth A. Bratton
Jacob C. Talley
Mary Ann Reynolds

Cyrus & Childers

1927

*Figure 1 The year Vivian Childers and Charles Cyrus married drop-waist
dresses were the latest ladies' fashion, Charles Lindbergh flew solo over the
Atlantic Ocean, Ford Model T cars were the rage and Calvin Coolidge was
President*

Table of Contents

Introduction

If you want to make a genealogist laugh, just ask her whether she's finished the family tree. The opportunities for exploration are endless: vital records, land records, photos, family stories, letters, local history, newspapers, etc. What makes this both fascinating and infuriating is that there is no central repository for all of these bits of information.

The family storytellers (aka genealogists) spend years just trying to gather bits of information and memorabilia. They spend weeks on end trying to organize it so that it can begin to tell a story. Inevitably, as the story begins to come together, big gaps in knowledge and confusing contradictions emerge.

As the obstacles develop, we quietly file away our stories and hope that eventually we'll stumble upon the answers we seek. Time passes, children are born, families grow, elders pass away, and our stories stay in a drawer.

This project is intended to pull together some of the stories that surround the family of Charles Cyrus and Vivian Childers. I never had the pleasure of meeting them. I married their grandson soon after they had both passed away. Their three daughters Carol, Shirley, and Jere worked hard to maintain a tradition of family reunions that has allowed the now large extended family to hold on to its history.

There have been many Cyrus family storytellers that I never met, but their memories and their research were handed down to me. Cinda Cyrus, Bill Cyrus, Jere Smith, and Shirley Mayer have all been conduits of precious family information. Not all of the source citations were handed down, but I've attempted to back track where I could, and identify information I have not been able to confirm. Nonetheless, you will find some portions have not been fully cited and therefore would not meet the Genealogical Proof Standard.

So, despite the fact that this history is now printed in a book, it will always be open to correction and additions. That is the essential nature of all historical accounts. Its value is in pulling together what several generations of Cyrus storytellers have carefully collected and recorded.

The initial inspiration for this project came from a slide show that was put together for Charles and Vivian's 60th wedding anniversary. The written script that accompanied the slide show was handed down with the slides. That is why this project is framed around Charles and Vivian.

All of us have two parents, four grandparents, and eight great grandparents. I have traced Charles and Vivian back to their great grandparents, but some lines are explored in greater detail than others. If you are descended from them, you will find family stories that date back to the early 1800's!

Most of the information about Charles and Vivian and their lives together was written by Shirley Cyrus Mayer. Most of the information about Charles and Vivian's ancestors was not part of the original slide show but was added from records that have been handed down and my own genealogical research.

If you hated your history classes, you'll be happy to know that Cyrus family history is not boring. Having met in Texas in the 1920's, Charles and Vivian descend from long lines of pioneers. I'll defer to Peter Falk's character in The Princess Bride, who comes to read a book to his grandson who is home sick.

The Grandson : A book?

Grandpa : That's right. When I was your age, television was called books. And this is a special book. It was the book my father used to read to me when I was sick, and I used to read

it to your father. And today I'm gonna read it
to you.
The Grandson : Has it got any sports in it?
Grandpa : Are you kidding? Fencing, fighting,
torture, revenge, giants, monsters, chases,
escapes, true love, miracles...
The Grandson : Doesn't sound too bad. I'll
try to stay awake.
Grandpa : Oh, well, thank you very much,
very nice of you. Your vote of confidence is
overwhelming.

Okay, so maybe the Cyrus story doesn't have all those
elements, but it does have cowboys, Indians, exploring new
lands, true love, fighting, heartache, and the everyday miracle
of families who do their best to make it all work.

Carla Whitacre Mayer
June 2019

Comments, corrections and additions can be sent to
bookmayer@me.com

Chapter One
Vivian Childers Marries Charles Cyrus
June 4, 1927

Two weeks after Charles A. Lindbergh flew The Spirit of St. Louis nonstop across the Atlantic Ocean, Charles Cyrus and Vivian Margaret Childers were married in Belton, Texas.

On June 4, 1927 the early southbound train from Cleburne arrived in Belton with a wedding bouquet specially made for Vivian by a family friend, Mrs. George Murphy. Beautiful white rose buds and delicate lilies-of-the-valley were ensconced in white satin ribbon.

The bride's white taffeta dress was just what she had envisioned when she ordered it in San Antonio. It had a long torso with a ruffled skirt – two-inch ruffles with picoted edges were sewn on one row after another. The dress came about three inches below the knee. Her short, bobbed hair peeked out from under a crushed band of white tulle with a 3-inch spray of orange blossoms on the right side.

At 10 a.m. Vivian's sister Gladys played "The Wedding March" on piano and the young bride came down the center aisle of First Baptist Church in Belton, Texas. Charles's favorite part of the service was when Gladys accompanied sister Leila playing "You Are My Song of Love" on the violin. Charles's brother, John, was best man and the only member of his family able to come to the wedding. Sadly, no pictures were taken that day, but Charles and Vivian recounted the day to their family often.

When the ceremony was over, Charles and Vivian planned to drive to Austin for summer school at University of Texas. Charles was careful to park his Ford Model T Coupe in a garage not far from the church with implicit instructions not to let anyone near his car until he returned. His brother John – always up for some mischief – not only talked his way past the workmen at the garage but got the workmen to help bedeck the rear bumper with cans, old shoes and, Charles said later, "other suitable junk." "All that stuff was a bumping and rattling as I went to pick up Vivian," Charles later recalled.

Vivian's sister Leila and a car full of well-wishers followed the couple about ten miles as they drove toward Austin – "a bumping and rattling" all the way. When the couple finally lost their tail, Charles pulled over and discovered the decorations were affixed to his bumper with heavy wire that had been tightly twisted. Always prepared,

Charles retrieved his pliers from his toolbox and sat by the side of road until the tokens of family love had been removed.

When they arrived in Austin, they went directly to Mick's Diner, near the Capitol grounds, and then walked to Zilker Park for a leisurely stroll.

Figure 2 Vivian Margaret Cyrus was born September 11, 1905

The wedding night was spent at Stephen F. Austin Hotel. Charles admitted he was alarmed when he woke up the next morning. "You must remember," Charles explains, "there was no air conditioning in those days. In the room was an electric fan that ran for an hour when one put in a dime. When we started getting up on Sunday morning, I discovered that Vivian had used three dimes during the night. I began to wonder – had I married a spendthrift?"

Through the years they have had much to learn about and from one another. Many of the elements of their wedding day, would be consistently present through their married years: airplanes, trains, beautiful flowers, stylish clothes, church, family, friends and fun adventures.

Like every couple, their story is the continuation of larger family stories. We're fortunate to have some of their stories and records that we want to be sure are preserved.

Part I: Vivian Childers' Roots

Chapter Two
Vivian Childers' Maternal Roots: The Capts

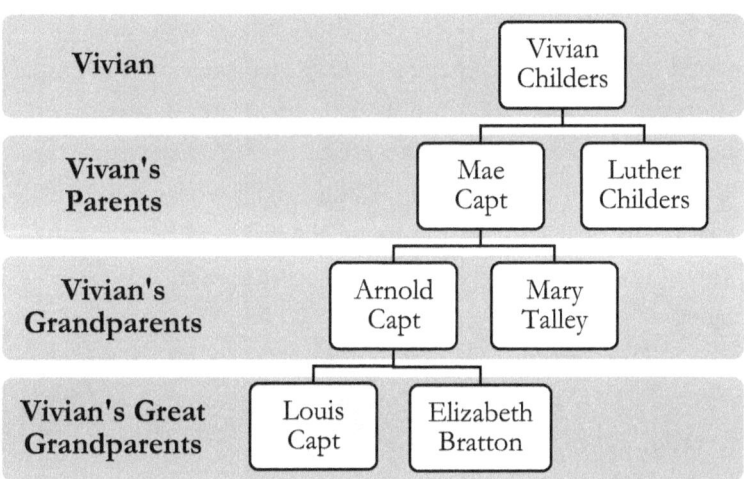

Vivian's Maternal Great Grandparents: Louis Capt and Elizabeth Bratton

Vivian's great grandfather Louis Capt was born on July 4, 1814 in Geneva, Switzerland.[i] There is an amazing story passed down in the family about Louis's circumstances before he came to the United States. According to Vivian, Louis studied at the University of Paris – also known as the Sorbonne. In one version of the story, he joined a class of students on a geological survey trip to Africa. Another version says he went with the Engineer professor on a field trip to Western Africa. The class ran into trouble with a native African tribe – the various versions of the story mention everything from slavery to cannibalism befalling the students.

All versions agree that Louis and at least one other classmate were not with the group at the time. In one version, Louis suffered sunstroke and was recovering nearby. When the men realized they were in danger, they set fire to a bog and scared off their captors. Another version says the men wooed their captors and eventually gained their own release. Whatever they did to escape their bad fortune, they are then said to have journeyed to the west coast of Africa where they "waved down a passing ship." Louis began working on the ships in the boiler room and made several trips between the United States and England before deciding to move to America.

This story is difficult, if not impossible, to verify. It was passed down within several branches of the family and one version was printed in *The Blanco County News* March 22, 1963 when a home that Louis once lived in became a historic landmark. Some in the family have speculated that a Swiss man named Bartel Schlitter, who is listed in the

Figure 3 Louis Capt on left and business partner Mr. Galbrith

1850 Census as living with Louis's family, might be the other classmate involved in Louis's African adventure.[ii]

Louis Capt's obituary merely states that "he traveled extensively over Europe," traveled to America in 1835, and to Texas in 1838. [iii] We don't know what brought Louis to Texas, but we do know that the US economy fell into a deep recession shortly after he arrived. Known now as the Panic of 1837, financial prospects were not good in most of the country, while Texas was offering free (or very cheap) land.

Advertisements like the one below beckoned settlers west.

Figure 4 Broadside Collection, BC_0258, The Dolph Briscoe Center for American History, The University of Texas at Austin

Of course, there was a catch. The early white settlers of Texas were not welcomed. They were intruding on land claimed by the Mexicans and Native American tribes, including Comanche, Lipan Apache, Kiowa and Ponca. When Louis arrived in Texas in 1838, he stepped into a world where settlers maintained a constant state of vigilance against threats to life and property. [iv]

Figure 5 Ponca Indian Meeting taken from Portal to Texas History website

No sooner had Texans finished fighting Mexico for independence, then brutal conflicts between settlers and Native Americans increased. They were at an all-time high in the 1830's and 1840's – just as Louis Capt settled in the area. Many violent encounters were recorded in Travis County where Louis settled. Judging by the brutal nature of the attacks, they appear to be intended to terrorize the early white settlers. One example is the story of two settlers who were shot by Native Americans and then, reportedly, "…the Indians scalped them, tore out their entrails and strewn them on the bushes around. They then cut off their arms, cut out their hearts…."[v]

In February 1841 Texas Land Commission offered land grants, known as head-right grants. Louis Capt wasted no time and applied April 21, 1841 for the 320 acres available to single men. His land grant was finalized in November 1845 when the Land Commission stated that he "has proven to us that he had been an actual resident of the Republic of Texas for the term of three years and that he has done and performed the duties required of him as such" (see Appendix)[vi] His land is described by the surveyor as being at the "head of the San Gabriel river" and northwest of Austin.[vii]

In 1843 Louis, now 28 years old, married 20-year-old Elizabeth Armstrong Bratton in Travis County Texas. Elizabeth was born in Wabach County, Indiana. It appears that Elizabeth's parents died before she was an adult, leaving her oldest brother John in charge of the family. John moved Elizabeth, age 15, and her siblings to Merrillville in Travis County in 1837.

The Bratton family emigrated from Ireland in the early 1700's. They have roots in Augusta County, Virginia where family members volunteered for the Virginia Militia in the Revolutionary War.

After Louis and Elizabeth were married, Louis opened a wheelwright and wagon-maker business on the corner of Congress Ave. and Sixth St. in Austin, Texas. This pen-and-ink sketch gives you some idea of the town that Louis adopted when he moved to Texas in the 1840's.

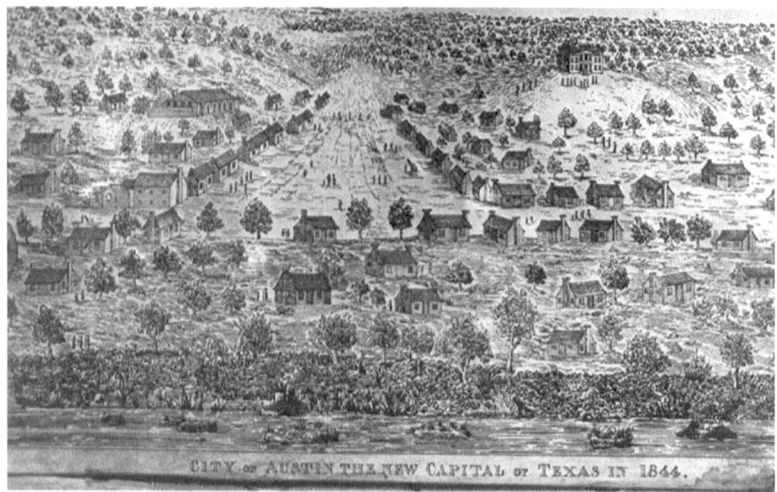

In census records Louis is listed as a mechanic (1850), farmer (1860), millwright (1870) and farmer (1880). Louis Capt built multiple grist mills throughout his life that all succumbed to flooding. His last mill was built about one mile upriver from Blanco. That mill was damaged by flood waters in July 1869 and then was completely destroyed by another flood in 1870[viii]. The family story is that Louis opened the mills as a public service and wouldn't charge people anything except a portion of the cornmeal they ground.

Louis's obituary says that Louis "spent considerable time with Big Foot Wallace, fighting the Indians."[ix] William Wallace was a well-known Texas Ranger who fought in the Mexican American War and then later formed groups to protect the early Texas settlers from Native American raids. The Adventures of Big Foot Wallace author John C. Duval quotes Wallace, giving us a flavor of the times:

In the fall of [18]42 the Indians were worse on the frontiers than they had even been before, or since. You couldn't stake a horse out at night with any expectation of finding him the next morning, a fellow's scalp wasn't safe on his head five minutes outside of his own shanty. The people on the frontiers at last came to the conclusion that something had to be done...so we...organized a company of about forty men and the next time the Indians came down from the mountains (and we hadn't long to wait for them) we took to the trail...[x]

We don't know specifically how and when Louis Capt was involved in fighting with Native Americans, but Louis's daughter Mary Louisa Capt West confirms that he did. In 1935 the local paper celebrated Mary's 82nd birthday.

Mrs. West, who was born June 24, 1853 on a ranch ...south of Austin... When she was a very young girl, the Indians were roaming through this country .... Quite often her brothers when bringing in the oxen were compelled to hide from the Indians when the Indians were too numerous to fight single-handed; on one occasion they had to hide in a wagon while the Indians were swarming about ; at another time the Indians stole their horses which were tied to her home. Those times were exciting as well as dangerous.[xi]

Figure 6 Known locally in Blanco as the Adrian Edwards Conn home, Louis Capt
and later his son A.W. Capt lived in this limestone house in the 1870's

By 1873 Capt moved to Blanco and moved into a
limestone house that was later recognized with a Texas
Historical Building Medallion (1962)[xii]. It's not known exactly
how long he lived there. It had two rooms on the ground level
and an attic room that was originally accessed by an outside
stairway.

Elizabeth died in 1888 and was buried in Blanco. She
was a proud Texan, including the date of her arrival in Texas
on her tombstone: Elizabeth Armstrong Capt; Born in Terre
Haute Ind. Nov. 13, 1822; Came to Texas 1837; Died
November 15, 1888. Louis lived almost another decade,
eventually moving in with his son Robert in Gonzales. Louis
died on May 7, 1897 at the age of 82 and is buried in
Gonzales.

Vivian's Maternal Grandparents: Arnold Winkelreid Capt and Mary Texana Talley

Louis and Elizabeth are believed to have had seven children, five boys and two girls. Their first-born son, William Tell Capt, enlisted in a Confederate regiment known as The Mounted Regiment in April 1863. He died in January 1864 at the age of 19 while still serving during the Civil War, but it is unknown whether he died from battle or disease.

William's younger brother (and Vivian's grandfather) Arnold Winkelreid Capt was only 14 when his older brother died. Arnold was born February 26, 1849. His unusual name is also the name of a famous 16th century Swiss war hero Arnold von Winkelreid. We don't know if Arnold's name was an homage to Louis's Swiss roots or if|Louis had another relative with that name in Switzerland.

Arnold was one of the early Texas cattle drivers and late in life was asked to write about his early experiences. His account, along with many others, is published in *Trail Drivers of Texas.*

Arnold was 12 years old when the Civil War began. Too young to serve, Arnold tells us he became a valuable resource to war widows and "any other folks where there was no one on the ranch that wore a pair of pants to ride the range and run in old 'Sooky' and any other cows or calves that could be penned."

Figure 7 Young Arnold Capt

Arnold attended a private secondary school in Hays County called The Johnson Institute. The original buildings were log cabins built by students[xiii]. Arnold felt too cramped in those surroundings and he left school before graduating.[xiv]

By the age of 21 he was driving large herds up the Chisholm Trail to Kansas. In 1871 he recounts a cattle drive that began from the branding pens on Williamson Creek. The trail boss arrived "bolstered up with a pillow in his saddle, having come in contact with the business end of a black steer at the branding pen, was almost out of commission." In addition to the trail boss, they had a cook, a horse wrangler, and sixteen cowboys to herd about 3,000 cattle.

"On the trail that year water was scarce, herds plentiful and dust more so." As they crossed the Colorado River below Austin, a stampede started, and the men fought to get control of the herd. When they finally got the last bovine over the river just before sunset, they realized the chuck wagon had been diverted to Austin for supplies and there would be no dinner. Capt comments wryly, "[Hunger] is a good appetizer; try it."

On a different cattle drive he recounts a dreadfully hot July day when one of the men "dropped back to the wagon and disrobed down to undershirt and drawers. He looked so cool that all tried the experiment, some leaving everything in the wagon." It turned out this particular hot July day was a

Sunday and they soon encountered "a whole camp meeting crowd of young ladies." Some of the cowboys rode off pretending to survey the prairie while others held their ground and tried to hide their embarrassment. Capt doesn't tell us which path he chose.[xv]

Figure 8 Arnold Winkelreid Capt

At 28, A.W. Capt married Mary Texana Talley, the youngest daughter of clergyman Jacob C. Talley, on April 19, 1877. Arnold and Mary lived in the limestone house originally purchased by Louis. The had their first two children Leila and Albert while living there. In 1882, with the arrival of their third child Mae (Vivian's mother) they seem to have decided the three-room limestone house was now too small and they sold it.

Arnold had a dry goods store on the west side of the town square across from the old courthouse in Blanco.

Mary contracted consumption (tuberculosis) in the spring of 1891 and died in August at the age 37.[xvi] Arnold now had six children to raise on his own. Leila, the oldest, was 13 and Bessie, the youngest, was less than a year old.

Leila took on many of her mother's duties at age 13 and remained an important maternal figure throughout her

Figure 9 Leila Capt cared for her younger siblings after her mother died.

life. She became a teacher and shepherded several relatives – including Vivian – into their teaching careers. She never married and seems to have cared for her father until he died in 1927 at the age of 77. She was asked once if she ever considered marriage, to which she reportedly replied, "Yes, but daddy needed me more."

Vivian's Mother: Mae Capt

Mae was only 9 years old when her mother died. Arnold kept the family together, kept the kids in school, and took in his father-in-law Jacob Talley in his old age.[xvii]

When Mae was 22 years old, she married Luther Childers at the Blanco Baptist Church in Blanco, Texas on August 24, 1904.[xviii] Luther was born and raised in Ripley, Mississippi. He moved to Blanco to live with his aunt Josephine Childers Weir. Josephine was widowed in 1903 with at least eight children at home. Luther was not interested in following his father into farming, and Aunt Josephine offered him a place to stay until he found a job.

Vivian remembers her mother Mae telling her a story about Luther and Mae's wedding picture.

In September 1904 after they'd been married in
August [and moved
from Blanco to San
Antonio]. My father
insisted that they
have a wedding
picture and he picked
a photographer in
San Antonio and
mother was to wear
her wedding dress.
They had company
come in from Blanco
-- Luther's cousin
Ivy. .... But [Ivy]
and mother were
very friendly, and

*Figure 10 Luther Childers and Mae
Capt's Wedding Picture*

they were having such a good time seeing each
other, having been parted about a month. They
were giggling and laughing and talking -- to my
father's distress. He was so provoked! He
wanted a dignified, serious wedding picture and
these two giggly girls were not only distracting
him but the photographer. [Luther] was angry
and mother finally got serious. [Mae] never
liked that picture because [Luther] was not a
very serious person and she knew how angry
he was. That picture always bothered her.[xix]

Luther worked in a furniture store on Commerce St. for
most of Vivian's childhood. When Vivian was in high school,
he was offered a job in banking and moved the family to
Elmer, Oklahoma.

Chapter Three
Vivian's Paternal Great Grandparents:
The Childers

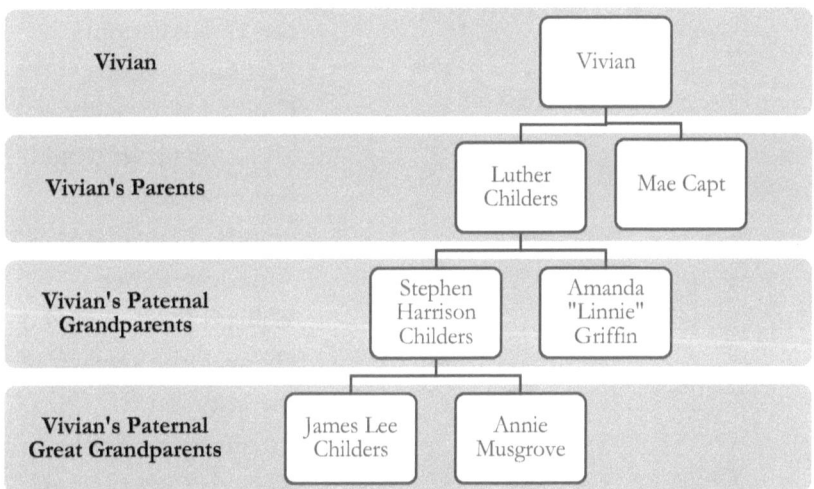

Vivian	Vivian	
Vivian's Parents	Luther Childers	Mae Capt
Vivian's Paternal Grandparents	Stephen Harrison Childers	Amanda "Linnie" Griffin
Vivian's Paternal Great Grandparents	James Lee Childers	Annie Musgrove

Vivian's Paternal Great Grandparents: James Lee Childers and Annie Musgrove

The Childers family line goes back to Virginia before the Revolutionary War. The son of the Revolutionary-War-era William Childers, Sr. ,William Childers, Jr.. fought in the War of 1812 and was given a land grant in Tennessee for his service.[xx] Vivian's paternal great grandfather, James Lee Childers was born in Williamson County, Tennessee in 1817. He married Annie Musgrove in 1839 and moved to Tippah County, Mississippi around 1845.

When James was 45 years old and his son, Stephen Harrison, was 16 they joined the Confederate Army Rangers. They enlisted August 1, 1862 in the 7th Mississippi Cavalry – also known as the 1st Mississippi Partisans -- under Colonel W.C. Falkner.

Falkner would become the great grandfather of famous American writer William Faulkner (who changed the spelling of the last name). Literature professor Renelda Owen, whose husband Billy Owen is a Childers' descendant, makes a convincing case that Faulkner's fictional Colonel Sartoris is based, in part, on the real-life commander. When William Faulkner writes in *Requiem for a Nun* that John Sartoris raised a Mississippi regiment "…not even a regiment yet but merely a voluntary association of untried men who knew they were ignorant and hoped they were brave…" it paints a picture of the challenge before James and Stephen Childers.

James's bravery was tested not long after he enlisted. James's grandson Tommy Stanford was interviewed in 1979 by Billy Owen about James's service in the Civil War. Owen printed the following account in The History of Tippah County[xxi].

> Military records show that on September 18, 1862, a skirmish was fought in Paden, Mississippi. The 2nd Iowa Cavalry about 1000 strong attacked the 1st Mississippi. Madison W. Smith was mortally wounded. His body fell into the road. James Childers refused to leave his friend's body and rode back to Smith. Childers was wounded in the process. He called for his wife and word was sent to her that her husband had been seriously wounded. Companions reported that he kept repeating, "Annie will come." Annie set out alone on horseback to tend to her wounded husband but arrived to learn that he had died only hours before she got to Paden.[xxii]

After James's death Annie makes a legal declaration in an effort to get the Confederate government to offer her financial help. She states that her husband served under Colonel Faulkner having enlisted "on or about 1st day of August 1862 having a wife and eleven children, that he died at Tishomingo on or about the 19th day of Sept. 1862 from wounds recved [sic] in Battle at Paytons Mill."[xxiii]

When the war ended in 1865, the federal government did not pay pensions for Confederate soldiers. More than 25 years later in 1888 the state of Mississippi began compensating Confederate widows. Mississippi records only four payments to an Annie Childers in Tippah County for approximately $20 per year. Somehow Annie still manages to raise her children and in 1900 at the end of her life we find her living with her youngest daughter Anna Louisa Hansford.[xxiv]

James Lee Childers and his friend, Smith, were buried at the battle site. Their remains were transferred to Ripley in 1977. James Childers is now buried at Jacob's Chapel Cemetery where he lies beside his wife who died August 14, 1904.[xxv]

Vivian's Paternal Grandparents: Stephen Harrison Childers and Amanda Linnie Griffin

Stephen Harrison Childers (Vivian's grandfather) survived the war. A Tippah County history says that he fought mostly in skirmishes in and around Virginia and after the war ended, "Steve and a friend, barefoot and hungry, walked from Virginia to their home in Ripley."

Already a war veteran by age 21, he married Amanda Melinda "Linnie" Griffin on December 28, 1866. Linnie was the daughter of Larkin Griffin, who was neighboring landowner. Larkin Griffin was born in Alabama in 1817 and served in the Mississippi 1st Cavalry during the Civil War.

James Lee Childers, Stephen's father, had owned a large farm (1100 acres) and Stephen took over the farm – presumably growing cotton. He owned and operated an early steam powered cotton gin that now resides at Union County Historical Museum.

Figure 11 Stephen (left) and Bill Garner in front of Stephen's house on Cotton Gin Road. His cotton gin was moved to the Union County Heritage Museum, New Albany, MS

Stephen and Linnie had twelve children. The fourth child, Luther Molver Childers married Mae Capt and their firstborn child was Vivian Margaret Childers.

Chapter Four
Mae Capt Marries Luther Childers and Vivian Childers is Born

Mae and Luther moved from Blanco to San Antonio about 1904. Vivian was born in San Antonio on September 11, 1905. Vivian was soon followed by sisters Leila, Gladys and Clarice. In the 1910 Federal Census Luther is listed as furniture salesman. The Childers and Capt families are shown together in a photograph that was probably taken around 1910.

Figure 12 Back row: Mae Childers, Albert Basil Capt, Beatrice Capt, Leila Capt, Bessie Bernice Capt, Arnold Earle Capt, Emmett Eugene Capt. Front row: Leila Childers, Luther Molver Childers holding Gladys Childers, Vivian Margaret Childers, Robert Bratton Capt, Evelyn M. Capt, Arnold E. Capt, A.W. Capt, and Bernice B. Capt.

By 1918, Luther's WWI registration (all men had to fill out a card whether or not they served) tells us the family had moved to Oklahoma with Luther working for the Bank of Elmer in Elmer, Oklahoma. Luther's brothers, Willie and Joe, and his sister Clara also settled in Oklahoma.

Vivian learned to sew at an early age and had a real knack for making her own clothes. She enjoyed tennis, playing with her Uncle Earl Capt every Sunday, and a local boy named Louie Biggs whenever she could. She liked school – especially before she moved to Oklahoma – and vied for the valedictorian spot with two of her male classmates. Leaving Breckenridge High School in San Antonio for Tipton, Oklahoma was a disappointment, but she graduated from Tipton High School in Oklahoma in 1922. Luther and Mae

Figure 13 Vivian Margaret Childers high school graduation picture

Childers had lofty goals for their daughters which included college degrees for all.

On September 27, 1922 Vivian entered Baylor Women's College with the largest freshman class to that time. Since Vivian's father Luther was a banker, he taught Vivian how to write checks from the family account to pay her bills. "I realized I was on my own to pay for my board and room and my tuition with my own checkbook. The excitement was over when I wrote the first check. It seemed so horrendous – so large that I feared my poor family wouldn't have enough left to buy groceries."[xxvi]

Luther had been watching the checks in the bank and knew that Vivian had only written one large check. In October Luther sent her a $5 bill and a sweet letter encouraging her to have some fun. At a time when girls were rigorously supervised and required to be in bed by 10 PM, Vivian and her roommates put their windfall to good use and finagled an after-hours party. This October letter from Luther would become even dearer to Vivian in retrospect because it would be the last letter she received from her father.

In November Luther was killed returning from an auction with a banking customer in his car. According to Vivian, the train tracks didn't have lights to warn you of a train, but it barely mattered since only one train a day went through town. Since it was well past time for the train, Luther didn't even stop at the tracks to look for the train. Unfortunately, the train was running late. The train struck Luther's car and killed him almost instantly. The coroner's office ruled it accidental.[xxvii]

The Daily Oklahoman printed this on November 29, 1922:

Tipton Banker is Killed
L.M. Childers Dies When Train Hits Automobile; Companion Hurt

Frederick, Nov. 28 – (special)-L.M. Childers, cashier of the Farmers State Bank of Tipton was killed and a companion, Huston

Stevens was slightly injured late Tuesday
afternoon when a sedan automobile in which
they were riding was run down by a southbound
Wichita Falls and Northwestern train. The
accident occurred on a crossing one-fourth mile
north of Tipton as Childers and Stevens were
returning from a farm sale, at which Childers
had been a clerk.

The Tillman Free Press (Frederick Oklahoma, November 30,
1922) reported that his car engine "went dead just as it
reached the track and being in an enclosed car it is likely that
in trying to get it started neither noticed the oncoming
passenger train until it was upon them. The car was struck
and thrown about twenty feet. It is believed the men were
thrown out of the car as neither of them were run over by the
train….Childers lived about fifteen minutes after being
struck." Vivian was only 17 years old when her father died.[xxviii]
        Judging from photographs, the funeral was an
elaborate affair. Some of the photos, no longer extant, are
said to have shown men in KKK regalia in the background of
some the photos. The Klan made a resurgence in the 1920's
attempting to rebrand itself as the protector of white
Protestantism, (and therefore anti-Catholic and anti-Jew). It
targeted local businessmen, such as Luther, for membership
and touted its Christian charity work. A front-page story in
1922 for a Thomas, Oklahoma newspaper read, "Klansmen
Visit Revival Meeting" and points out that the Klan left two
crisp $10 bills to defray the cost of the meeting and left a note
stating that "Bootleggers, gamblers, and unscrupulous men"

were warned to watch their step because the Klan promised to protect "the chastity of their young women."

The backlash was swift and the resurgence of the KKK began to wane again within a few years. If Luther was involved in the KKK, he did not live long enough to see the backlash and we don't know if he would have chosen to stay or break with the group as its veneer of moral fortitude was stripped away.

Figure 14 Funeral of Luther Molver Childers, 1922. Pictures of the burial are said to have included some KKK members dressed in regalia, but those pictures have since been lost or discarded.

After Luther's death, Mae worked hard to get her daughters through college. This meant a move to Belton, Texas, where Mae Childers became a house mother in a dorm to help pay tuition for her four daughters to attend Baylor Women's College now Mary Hardin Baylor University.

In a letter between Luther's brothers Willie and Eskar, Willie says "Maye [sic] is making a desperate struggle to educate the girls and is working day and night to keep them in school; they are taking a good education and doing well."[xxix]

Vivian graduated in 1925. Vivian's list of college activities includes baseball and tennis, as well as several clubs including the Education Club.

After college, Vivian moved back to San Antonio to live with Aunt Leila Capt. Aunt Leila and her brother Earl

were both single and lived at 245 East Lotus Street, San Antonio. They welcomed Vivian and her sisters Gladys and Leila as all the women worked as teachers. Uncle Earl is listed as a building manager in the 1930 Census, but eventually became a pharmacist.[xxx]

The toll of Luther's death on Mae is reflected much later in a letter she wrote to her sister-in-law Mazie in 1951 after Mazie's husband died. Mae says, " I'm sure you know I truly can sympathize with you, tho, it has been twenty-eight years since I was called to endure the same sorrow…that heartache is still there. I am lonely and wish for Luther…As I'm sure you [know] I had depression after Luther was taken…."

Figure 15Mae Childers in Baylor's 1926 Yearbook. She is listed as the Hostess of Ruth Stribling Hall.

After Vivian and her sisters were grown, Mae lived with her older sister Leila, who had retired from school teaching. Mae writes in her letter to Mazie that she didn't want to be a burden to her children, and she was grateful for Leila's companionship. Mae writes, "I'm glad to be with her. "[xxxi]

Figure 16 Leila Capt

Part II

Charles Cyrus's Roots

Figure 17 Jennie Ball Cyrus with daughter Jennie and son Charles

Chapter Five
Charles Cyrus's Maternal Roots: The Balls

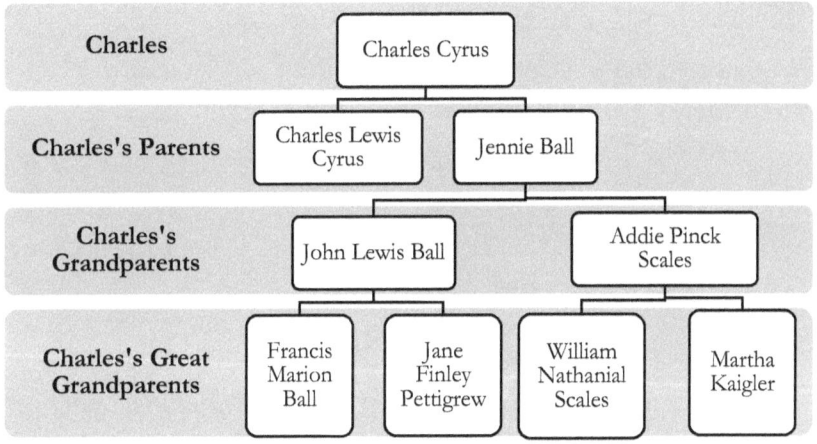

Charles's Maternal Great Grandparents: Francis Marion Ball and Jane Finley Pettigrew

Now that we know something about Vivian's roots, we can look more closely at Charles Cyrus's roots. His mother was Jennie Lewis Ball. The Ball family has a long history as American pioneers. The family lived in Virginia prior to the Revolutionary War. There are at least two Ball genealogy lines in Virginia during the 1700's. Sometimes referred to as the "rich Balls" and the "poor Balls"[xxxii], one of these family lines boasts the mother of George Washington, Mary Ball. However, since many men in both lines had common names such as William Ball or John Ball, I am now convinced that Virginia Ball genealogy is where genealogists go to die.

What we do know is that some of the Virginia Balls moved to South Carolina[xxxiii]. We also know that Charles Cyrus's great grandfather Francis Marion Ball was in a position to buy 240 acres of land in Tuscaloosa, Alabama in 1834 and another 400 acres in 1837. The Land Act of 1820 lowered the price of western land from$2.00 an acre to $1.25 an acre. The only catch was that credit was no longer available. Land had to be paid for up front.

Charles's Maternal Grandparents: John Lewis Ball and Addie Pinck Scales

Francis Marion Ball married Jane Finley Pettigrew in 1836 and soon after pushed west again to Winston County, Mississippi. Charles Cyrus's grandfather John Lewis Ball was born in Winston County, Mississippi in 1840.

In early 1861, rising tension between North and South was about to kick off what we now know as The Civil War. In the months leading up to the attack on Fort Sumter, most believed the hostilities would only last a few months. John Ball signed up for his state militia-- the 13th Mississippi Infantry -- with his two younger brothers less than three weeks before Fort Sumter.

John Ball was 20 years old when he enlisted on March 16, 1861 in Louisville, Mississippi. We don't know the specific circumstances of John's enlistment but an enlistment account of R. N. Rea, a private in the same company and regiment as John Ball, paints a picture of the fervor surrounding the coming war. Rea explains:

When Mississippi seceded from the Union in
1861, I was a boy of fifteen and half years of
age, a student of Marion High School which
was composed of young men and boys. When
school convened the next day following this
important event in history of our country, our
professor promptly dismissed us and our
schoolbooks were closed forever. Our school
was organized into a company with our teacher
as Captain…"[xxxiv]

Frustrated that they were not immediately mustered into
service, Rea's says they took "French leave" (slang for going
away without permission) and joined Company A of the 13th
Mississippi Regiment.

The first major battle for the 13th Mississippi was the
Battle of Bull Run on July 2, 1861. They would go on to fight
in more than two dozen major battles, including Manassas,
Antietam (Sharpsburg), Leesburg, Gettysburg, Seven Pines,
Chickamauga, and The Battle of the Wilderness.

Historian John McLean says, what the men expected
to last a few months, "… turned into almost five years during
which, [the 13th Mississippi Infantry] will walk, freeze, sweat,
battle, bleed and die across Virginia, Pennsylvania, Maryland,
Georgia and Tennessee."[xxxv]

The fighting for John Ball ended on July 2, 1863 at
Gettysburg, three long years after he enlisted. In the heat of
the battle, the Confederates were being beaten down by
Union forces under General Sickles, and Confederate Colonel
Barksdale was apoplectic on the sidelines, waiting for his unit
to be called into the battle. When he was finally allowed to

Figure 18 John Lewis Ball

lead the 13th Mississippi into battle, his unit was fierce – almost pushing through the Union line.

One of the Union colonels said "…it was the grandest charge ever made by mortal man." Many considered this attack to be the high-water mark for the Confederates at Gettysburg. The drama of this scene is captured in a painting by Mort Kunstler called "The Grandest Charge Ever Seen" that was hanging in The Gettysburg Museum when I visited in 2014. The artist's estate would not grant permission to include it in this book, but I would encourage you to search for it online. It shows the 13th Mississippi regimental flag unfurled as William Barksdale – hat raised in the air – goads his men to victory.

John Ball and his brother William were wounded in the battle. William's service records states bleakly "Wounded at Gettysburg July 2, 1863. Left in enemy line."

John and William Ball were taken to a Union hospital on David's Island, New York. John suffered a gunshot wound, which shot away part of his right knee cap. The story passed down through John's daughter-in-law Empriss Jowell Ball is that John was told his leg was going to be amputated. He vociferously objected and refused any anesthesia while under treatment for fear they would remove it in spite of his wishes. The doctors respected his stamina and his wish to study medicine, so they agreed to forego the operation and to do everything in their power to help him toward recovery.

Four months after Gettysburg, he was released into Confederate hands. He was discharged from active duty May 9, 1865 and reassigned as a clerk. His medical discharge papers say he then suffered from gangrene. His injuries impaired his ability to flex and extend his leg.[xxxvi] (see Appendix for a copy of his discharge certificate)

John's brother, William, survived Gettysburg but was killed in action less than a year later at the Battle of Hanover Junction. (John would name his first son after his brother William). Jasper, the third brother serving with the 13th Mississippi was on sick leave during the battle of Gettysburg but was wounded in the particularly brutal Battle of the Wilderness on May 6, 1864 and had to have his right foot amputated.

When John Ball returned from the war, he married Addie Pinck Scales on February 25, 1869 in Mississippi. Her parents, William Nathaniel Scales and Martha Kaigler, were both from families of large plantation owners. Addie grew up wealthy with servants (slaves) to do her bidding. William Nathaniel Scales and his brothers would have had hundreds of slaves in their service before the Civil War. You can find a more detailed discussion of this in "The Scales Slaves" in the appendix.

Addie's father, William Nathaniel Scales, was a
Confederate prisoner of war
at Camp Chase, Ohio where
he contracted erysipelas, a
strep infection of the skin
also known as St. Anthony's
fire. He died April 9, 1864
when Addie was only 12
years old. Addie's mother
Jane raised the three
children, ran the plantation
and managed to send Addie
to Columbia Athenaeum
College in Columbia, Tennessee.

Figure 19 Addie Pinck Scales

Many of Addie's uncles had distinguished careers after
the Civil War, including Alfred Moore Scales, who became the
governor of North Carolina.

John Ball achieved his dream to be a medical doctor.
In 1967, John's daughter-in-law Empriss Jowell Ball compiled
a history titled "History of the Dr. John Lewis Ball Family"
(see appendix). In it, she says that John Ball started his
education as a pharmacy clerk in a Louisville drugstore,
studying medicine at night. After the Civil War, he attended
Louisville Kentucky Medical College and began his practice in
Greenwood Mississippi.[xxxvii]

The couple spent their first few years in Mississippi
and gave birth to their first child, William (Buddy). In 1872
they became concerned about a malaria outbreak in the area
and made the decision to move to Texas. Two of John Ball's
brothers moved with them to Calvert, Texas. Still plagued by
yellow fever and malaria in Calvert, John and Addie Ball , now

with three children, moved to a higher altitude, buying a farm in Johnson County, Texas in 1876.

John eventually specialized in obstetrics. The medical profession was far less prestigious at the time than it is now. According to family history, Addie decided she didn't want John touching other women and he eventually settled into farming. Despite this career change, she always called him, "Dr. Ball", and he wore his customary professional attire -- stiffly starched white collared shirt and a black bow tie every day even when he was pushing a plow in the fields.

Charles Cyrus's Mother: Jennie Lewis Ball

By 1888, John and Addie had seven children. One girl, Jennie Lewis Ball, (Charles Cyrus's mother) and six boys. In 1888 the Ball family intended to have their picture taken one Sunday after church. The photographer was late for the photo session and the younger boys had already changed into play clothes. In the picture below, John and Addie Ball stand with their seven children. Charles Cyrus' s mother, Jennie Lewis Ball, (on the left) was 15 years old at the time. She was the second oldest child and the only girl. Jennie Lewis Ball, like her mother Addie, was among those first waves of women to attend college in the United States. Her older brother William, known as Buddy, studied medicine at Baylor College in Waco, Texas.

Jennie was allowed to follow him and attend Baylor Women's College. Records for Jennie's Fall 1890 semester tells us she studied trigonometry, botany, rhetoric, elocution, geometry algebra, geology and Texas history. Women were new to the college scene, so instead of receiving a Bachelor of Science, her 1892 diploma refers to her as a "Maid of Science".[xxxviii] When she returned to Cleburne Texas she was selected as the young lady to represent Johnson County at the World's Fair being held in Chicago in 1893. Buddy accompanied her on this exciting trip. When she returned, she

Figure 20 Jennie Lewis Ball

became a teacher. Throughout the rest of her life, she is mentioned often in her local newspaper for performing readings and dramatic recitations at community events – she was certainly well-known in Cleburne.

In 1894 at the age 24 Jennie Lewis Ball married Charles Lewis Cyrus, Sr.

Chapter Six
Charles Cyrus's Paternal Roots: The Cyrus's

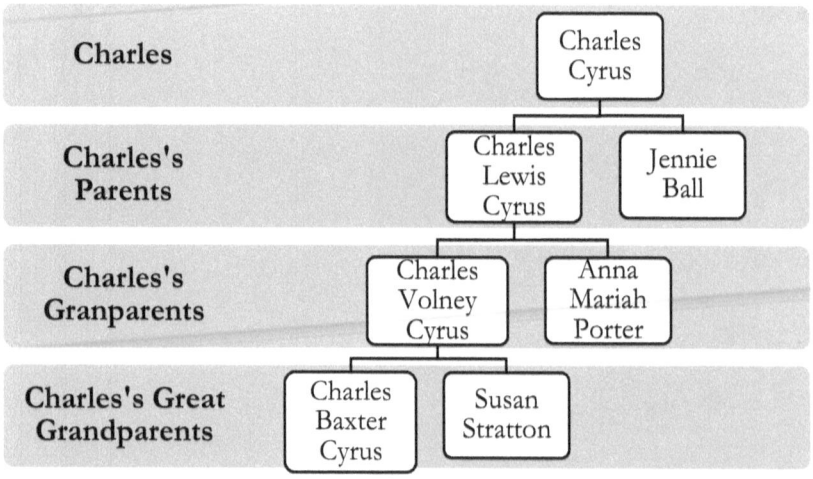

Charles		Charles Cyrus
Charles's Parents	Charles Lewis Cyrus	Jennie Ball
Charles's Granparents	Charles Volney Cyrus	Anna Mariah Porter
Charles's Great Grandparents	Charles Baxter Cyrus	Susan Stratton

Charles Cyrus's Great Grandparents: Charles Baxter Cyrus and Susan Stratton

Like the Ball family, Charles Cyrus's paternal side of the family were pioneers. Charles Cyrus's great, great grandfather was Henry Cyrus. He is recorded marrying Peggy Connor on October 10, 1810 in Logan, Kentucky. Henry shows up in the court minutes when he is ordered to apprentice George Robertson (presumably orphaned) in "art and mystery of the saddler's trade"[xxxix]

In 1812 their only known child, Charles Baxter Cyrus is born. Logan County, KY has no further records of Henry, but a later biography of Henry's grandson Charles Volney Cyrus says that Henry served in the War of 1812 and was killed in Pensacola, Florida in 1814 under General Andrew Jackson.[xl]

Little is known about Charles Baxter Cyrus other than he married Susan Stratton in 1838 and moved to Maury County, Tennessee. Charles dies at the age of 44 with only two known children: Charles Volney Cyrus and Virginia Victoria Cyrus.

Charles's Paternal Grandparents: Charles Volney Cyrus and Anna Mariah Porter

Charles Volney Cyrus (Charles's grandfather) was

born May 28, 1840 in Giles County, Tennessee. When he is 21 years old he enlisted in the Confederate 9th Battalion Tennessee Cavalry. Three months later his entire battalion was captured by Ulysses S. Grant at Fort Donelson. C.V. Cyrus was imprisoned at Camp Morton, Indiana for 6 months. His battalion was freed at prisoner exchange at Vicksburg in September of 1862.

Figure 21 Anna Mariah Porter

Once released, C.V. Cyrus and the rest of the battalion rode horseback for a month to join their unit in Port Hudson near Baton Rouge, Louisiana. He was captured again on November 11, 1863 and remained a prisoner of war until May 1865. His longest stay as prisoner was a full year at Fort Delaware.

When C.V. Cyrus returns from the war, he marries Anna Mariah Porter on September 1, 1869. He is an active member of both the Methodist Episcopal Church, South and the Democratic Party. He is elected to serve in the 47th General Assembly 1891 -1892. While serving in the state legislature, C.V. Cyrus is said to have championed the establishment of a home for Confederate veterans on the grounds of The Hermitage, Andrew Jackson's home in Nashville Tennessee. Jackson's home was preserved as a museum and a new building was constructed on the grounds to house 125 veterans. It operated from 1892 until 1933.

C.V CYRUS. Maury Co

Charles's Father: Charles Lewis Cyrus

C.V. and Anna Mariah Cyrus had eight children. The oldest was Charles Lewis Cyrus (Charles's father) born September 12, 1870 in Maury County, Tennessee. Charles Lewis and his younger brother William James move to Cleburne, Texas circa 1890. They bought land on N. Buffalo St and began building a house for their parents and siblings. When the house was finished, the entire family moved to

Texas. Charles Lewis started a business handling feed, grain, and coal, which he bought by the train car load.[xli]

Figure 22 Charles Lewis Cyrus

Chapter Seven
Jennie Ball Marries Charles Lewis Cyrus:
Charles Cyrus is Born

Jennie Lewis Ball and Charles Lewis Cyrus were
married June 15, 1898. After the wedding, they moved into a
home lovingly built by Charles Lewis at 702 Featherstone
Street, Cleburne. Their daughter Addie (named after Jennie's
mother) described a one-and-a-half story, gingerbread house,
with Victorian trim. It had lots of extra touches, like two
stained glass windows, a built-in drainboard in the kitchen,
and -- Addie's favorite -- a built-in china closet in the
wainscoted dining room. (See appendix for Addie's full
account.)

Despite Charles's
efforts to woo Jennie,
Jennie's mother Addie Ball
opposed the marriage,
telling Jennie, "If you
marry Charlie Cyrus, I will
never enter your house."
Addie stayed true to her
word. Addie's objections
are not recorded but we
do know that "Charlie"
was a Methodist, and the
Ball family was Southern
Baptist. In this day and
age, it's hard to imagine such a difference would cause strife

Figure 23 Charles Cyrus about 1900

in a family, but it was not unusual at the turn of the 20th century.

Charles Lewis and Jennie had five children: Charles, Jennie, John, Addie, and Ralph. Charles, who later married Vivian, was born May 6, 1899. Charles Lewis Cyrus will be referred to as Charles Lewis to avoid confusion with his son, also named Charles.

One of Charles's first memories is from 1906. Then, 7-year-old Charles remembers an airplane landing near Cleburne, Texas. "The boys brought the family milk cows for pasture during the daytime…Three of us were down there and we heard an airplane. Here it comes. It was a bi-plane with the pilot sitting in the open. He landed nearby in the cow pasture. We ran over to see the airplane. He had run out of gas. 'Will you boys keep the milk cows off my plane while I go get some gas?' …When he returned…[w]e held the end of the wings back until he got the engine revved up; then we stepped back and up he went." [xlii]The boys got a nickel for their troubles and a great story to tell their family and friends.

Figure 24 Charles took his first automobile ride on the back of a car like this one.

Automobiles were still fairly rare at the time. Horse and buggies were the usual mode of transportation. Charles remembers his first ride in an automobile. The dentist's wife, Mrs. Streetman, came puffing along unpaved Forest Avenue in Cleburne in a car with a side-crank engine and tiller to steer. When she noticed Mr. Cyrus's little boy standing by the side of the road with his mouth hanging open, she asked him if he wanted a ride. He jumped up and sat on a square box situated behind the seat in the open-air car and proudly rode three or four blocks before Mrs. Streetman had to turn off the road. Charles ran the rest of the way home yelling, "I rode on an automobile!"

Charles's mother Jennie worked hard and expected her children to do likewise. One day when 11-year-old Charles was in school, a runner came from the office with the alarm that there had been a phone call for Charles, and he should get home at once.

> I took off running mostly; and when I got to the house I entered (we never locked anything) calling "Mom, Mom!" and went on thru finding mom washing in the backyard. The usual set up was the boiling wash pot with soapy water and two rinse tubs, and final bluing tub (to make the clothes whiter). I said, "Mom did you phone for me?"
>
> "Yes! Go hang up your pajamas!"

Charles said he hung up his pajamas every day for the rest of his life.

The big pot that was used for laundry had many important functions for the family. For instance, it was used to heat scalding water to loosen the hair on a hog at hog killing time. It was also used to cook down the excess fat from the hog to render it into lard. The pot sat on three short legs situated on top of flat bricks; leaving room for the fire underneath.

When Charles was in 7th grade, he was assigned the task of tending to a large pot of fat that was being rendered into lard. " For hours, I stirred, fired, and breathed those fumes from the hot fat. Shortly after midnight, I became very sick"

Charles called for his mother, who used a homemade mixture that included turpentine, kerosene, hog lard and mineral oil as a chest-rub and sat him close to the coal-burning fireplace.

Charles's condition worsened into pneumonia and an abscess developed on his lung. This was before the invention of antibiotics, and such illnesses were extremely serious.

Jennie called her brother William (known as Buddy) who was the local doctor. Buddy arrived at the house with an assistant and operated on Charles at home. The kitchen table was cleared and placed before the fireplace. Buddy inserted drainage tubes into Charles's lungs to drain fluid from his lungs.

Charles had a long recovery. Charles remembers, "Buddy had set up two 5-gallon bottles with pink water, rubber tubing and glass fittings, and for weeks I had to blow that water from one bottle to the next." He first became ill in February of 1913 and did not fully recover until the start of school in the fall – about six months.

From the time Charles was a young boy until he was in his 20's, he worked for his grandmother Addie Ball. She took in boarders after the children left home, so young

Charles would go to her house and help with cleaning, sweeping, and dusting, as well as bringing in coal and wood. She sold eggs and butter to the neighbors, so Charles cleaned out the hen house and the cow stall. He earned 15 cents an hour and had to keep his own time sheet. In many ways she was a hard task master, but Charles said it made him a better worker. [xliii]

Jennie and Charles Lewis Cyrus Divorce

Problems existed between Jennie and Charles Lewis for most of Charles's childhood. Their daughter Addie suggests that the problems may have begun in 1905, when Charles Lewis contracted typhoid fever and almost died. Soon after Charles lost his business and struggled to make a living farming. One of the long-term effects of typhoid can be psychiatric problems, including delirium and paranoia – which some in the family have suggested was the case with Charles.

Whatever the contributing factors, Jennie filed and was granted a divorce May 25, 1918. The divorce decree states that "the court finds that the material facts alleged in the plaintiffs petition are true, and that plaintiff is entitled to a divorce." The decree does not tell us the "material facts."

Jennie's daughter Addie Cyrus tells of an incident with her older brother Charles. The elder Charles intended to discipline his son with a switch, but according to Jennie, the "switch" was a tree limb. Jennie intervened to protect the younger Charles and the incident remained a sore spot for all involved. After that, Addie only remembers corporal punishment being administered by her mother.

Addie Cyrus recalls sweet moments with her father, like sitting and talking while they ate apples out of an apple barrel her father kept in his room. When Addie was about eleven years old, she was told that her parents had divorced, and that dad was leaving.

When the day came, she says she was standing on the porch with her siblings. "Mom and Dad were in the yard just below us. They were both calm. We said goodbye. He stood there a bit longer with no other words; then turned and walked away. There were no tears, no kisses, only silence. Nobody moved for several minutes, then slowly and quietly we scattered."[xliv] You can read Addie's full account in the appendix.

Charles Cyrus

Charles Cyrus was already 19 years old when his parents divorced. Charles dropped out of school to help his family financially. He became a machinist apprentice on the Santa Fe Railroad (1922). As a machinist apprentice he was paid 17.5 cents an hour. Apprentices worked 10 hours a day and, "all the overtime the men could take." Charles describes his work.

> A steam locomotive is a boiler set on wheels which are the engine. The whole contraption was held together with bolts. (It was before the invention of electric arc welding). As well as working full time in the shop, the apprentices

went to shop school four [days] a week studying shop arithmetic and mechanical drawing. In the big flu epidemic of 1918, I did not get sick as so many of the shop men. I made bolts for eight months, and I was put on a drive wheel axle lathe when the journeyman got sick. Normally, apprentices were not permitted to run such. As the war continued, when the 19-year-olds were required to register for military service, I was directed to stay on the job at the shop as I could be more serviceable there than as a new recruit[xlv]

After WWI ended, Charles finished his apprenticeship and began working as a full-fledge machinist making 75 cents an hour working as a lathe operator.

On July 4, 1922 the railroad union went on strike. When Charles informed his mother, she said, "Good! You can go back to school!" After some summer tutoring, he returned to high school in the fall of 1922.

He got his high school diploma the following spring in May 1923 and worked as a machinist at the Texaco

Figure 25 Charles Cyrus as a young man

Oil Refinery in Port Arthur, Texas -- all before he began his college career at Texas A&M and then University of Texas.

Work on the railroad gave Charles an appreciation for trains that lasted the rest of his life. His machinist certificates gave him the ability to teach school before he had accumulated many college credits. A teaching job in San Antonio the fall of 1925 set the stage for Charles and Vivian to meet.

Figure 26 Charles Cyrus still enjoying trains in his senior years

Chapter Eight
Charles Cyrus and Vivian Childers' Romance

Charles and Vivian met the first time either of them attended a Baptist Young People's Union gathering at First Baptist Church in San Antonio in October of 1925. Charles was living at the YMCA and Vivian was living with her Aunt Leila at 245 Lotus Street.

After the meeting, Charles volunteered to escort Vivian to a church service at Travis Park Methodist Church and then they caught a streetcar back to Aunt Leila's. When they arrived, Vivian was so thrilled to discover that her mother and sisters had come to visit, that Charles seems to have quietly slipped away. Fortunately, he had managed to get Vivian's phone number and that night marked the beginning of their courtship.

After sitting together at church many times, Charles asked Vivian to go out to dinner at a fancy restaurant named *Manhattan* on Houston Street. The menu was in French, which neither of them could read, so the waiter steered them toward a Welsh Rarebit entrée. They both tried to conceal their surprise when it arrived in a flaming chaffing dish – the memory of which made them giggle whenever they recalled it.

A year later, in the fall of 1926, Charles moved to a neighboring house on Lotus St. to be close to Vivian. Apparently, he did not consult Vivian, because she was not pleased. Her comings and goings were none of his business. Furthermore, when her tennis buddy Louie Biggs came to the house he would sometimes run into Charles – making for some awkward interactions. Vivian was relieved a few months later when Charles got a job and moved to Ft. Worth, Texas.

They continued their courtship long distance. Charles drove from Fort Worth to San Antonio in his Model T Ford Coupe to visit Vivian. Charles described his trip.

It was 300 miles between Fort Worth and San Antonio. The road was mostly graveled, it ran along farm fence lines, made square turns at the corners, and went through the middle of all towns and villages enroute. It was a 12-hour drive each way. I would leave Fort Worth at the end of school on payday Friday, and plan to get back to school by school-time on Monday morning. Mrs. [Mae] Childers lived in Belton, Texas. I would get there about bedtime as I drove south, and she would take me to the ice room for something to eat. I would carry any messages or anything to go as I went on [driving through the night]. I would get to San Antonio in time to sleep a few hours on the couch before we would start Saturday activities.

Charles was a dedicated suitor and Vivian's Grandfather Capt encouraged her not to let him get away.

Early Married Years

Charles and Vivian began their married life in 1927 going to summer school at the University of Texas. Living in the shadow of the UT tower was to be prophetic because they ended up spending most of their married life near UT. Their first apartment was on Fifth Avenue across a driveway from a mortuary. The ambulance would leave with full siren blowing and not wake Charles and Vivian. When the ambulance returned from a run and backed into its garage with the

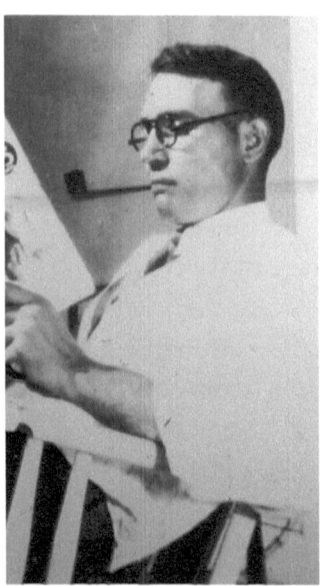

engine racing it would wake them up.

A photographer friend, Garner Adams, documented their first three apartments during those early days when Charles smoked a pipe and looked like a true intellectual. A brief detour by Texas A&M for Charles to obtain his B.S. degree in 1930 gave him the document to back up his scholarly look.

Then Carol Ruth and Shirley May joined the family while Charles and Vivian were living at the farm next door to Charles's mother, Jennie Ball Cyrus. That farm is now part of the Dallas/Ft. Worth International Airport.

Charles was offered a teaching position with the Division of Extension at The University of Texas and the

family moved to Austin in December of 1934. Carol was
about to turn 2 years old and Shirley was only 6 weeks old.

Figure 27 Charles and Vivian Cyrus about 1927

The first house was on Blanco St. Later, they moved
to Red River, across the street from the UT baseball field and
the Texas Memorial Museum. Shirley could see the field from
her window and once fell out of a second-floor window while
watching a ball game! Fortunately, a bush broke her fall, so
she walked away unscathed.

The most memorable piece of furniture in the house
was a genuine wooden ice box that would be a collector's item
today. It was great fun to get chips of ice to suck on when the
ice man delivered the block of ice each week. Today that
house has been replaced by the Lyndon B. Johnson
Presidential Library.

Charles and Vivian then made the move to 1703
Linscomb to the house that would be home for over fifty
years. They got a great buy for a 2-bedroom, 1- bathroom,
white frame house with a large backyard. It was situated on a

bluff above Barton Creek in South Austin. One prerequisite was that the house not be on the Colorado River flood plain, which flooded periodically. The girls were not old enough to request a house within walking distance of the "greatest swimming pool on earth" but this also was an advantage of 1703 Linscomb. It was located near Barton Springs.

Figure 28 1703 Linscomb Rd., Austin, Texas

Chapter Nine
The Growing Years

Keeping up with three growing daughters did not consume all Charles and Vivian's time and energies. Charles's job in those days, was traveling all over the state of Texas "teaching teachers how to teach." He worked for the Department of Industrial Education (later, The Division of Extension) at the University of Texas where he focused specifically on teachers who taught trades.

While Charles traveled, Vivian held down the fort at home. She sewed clothes for the girls, served as PTA President of Becker Elementary School, as well as other neighborhood groups – including a book club and a hook-rug club.

Figure 29 Jere, Shirley and Carol Cyrus

The women enjoyed being together and getting out of the house so much that both groups continued to meet together for over 13 years.

When Charles was home from his travels the yard took much of his spare time. He took unattractive areas near the driveway and created flower beds that beautified the neighborhood. He planted Georgia sugarcane and bamboo in strategic places for shade and privacy. He loved irises, miniature roses and he grew a prize-winning variety of daylilies. Vivian became an expert at flower arranging and entered flower show competitions.

The backyard was also a laboratory for experimental activities, such as bee keeping. Extracting the honey was a major undertaking, but family and neighbors enjoyed the fruits of the labor.

Figure 30 Built by Charles Cyrus, this playset was known as "the acting bars" because it was where the girls would show off - Charles is clearly getting into the act here.

The girls enjoyed playing on a sturdy children's trapeze set affectionately called "the acting bars" because the girls liked to use it to show off. The Cyrus girls and most of the 13 grandchildren have enjoyed seeing what they could do on the inclining ladder

Even with all of Charles and Vivian's activities, they firmly believed in exposing their girls to enriching experiences such as travel, camping and canoeing – doing these as a family, if possible.

Figure 31 Shirley and Carol Cyrus

Because Charles traveled by car so much for his job, a vacation for him was not more car travel. However, his love for camping and seeing the USA enabled him to endure family car vacations to Big Bend country and later to the Tetons. While we enjoyed the marvelous scenery, we didn't always enjoy the effort it took to freshen up each day. Our main resource for a shower was at public swimming pools.

The most dramatic event was when Charles single handedly turned the door of the 75 lb. tent around 180 degrees in the middle of a sandstorm. The beauty of the Tetons made those extra efforts worthwhile.

Canoeing was another love of Charles which he shared with his girls. (He would later give each girl a canoe as a wedding present.) It was with great pride that the Cyrus clan paddled Jere to Camp Texlake the summer of 1953. The day was marred only by one thing: the noon picnic was mayonnaise sandwiches.

Chapter Ten
Family Growth

Figure 32 Charles and Vivian in their living room on Linscomb Ave, ready for the wedding of Carol to Glen Zumwalt in 1952

While Carol studied zoology at the University of Texas, she met Glen Zumwalt. Glen, six and a half years older than Carol, had served in the Navy in WWII and was able to use the G.I. Bill to come to University of Texas. Carol was responsible for planning summer activities for incoming freshman at University Baptist Church. Glen was her first and most enthusiastic participant. They married December 21, 1952 in Austin, Texas when Carol was still a sophomore in college. When she graduated, Carol and Glen moved to

University of Illinois (Urbana) for Glen to start a PhD program in Mechanical Engineering. Glen went on to become a professor at Oklahoma State University and Wichita State University.

Shirley graduated from University of Texas in 1956 with a major in Elementary Education. She met Dave Mayer at Campus in the Woods in Canada. It was an Intervarsity Christian Fellowship's camp for leadership training. They became engaged to be married at Urbana where Dave was also student. It was so convenient to have the Zumwalts there so Shirley and Dave could practice on the first Cyrus grandchild, Marylee Zumwalt. Dave, born in Illinois, would become the first Yankee in the family.

Figure 33 Dave and Shirley Mayer holding Marylee Zumwalt

Jere studied nursing at University of Texas, but her major required her to transfer to the Galveston campus for her last two years. In fall of 1963, her suite mate suggested Jere as a date for an old high school friend, Jack Smith. Jack was studying at the Maritime Academy at Texas A& M. Their

first date was to an A&M football game. The couple married
September 1965 and settled in Galveston, Texas.

*Figure 34 Shirley and Dave Mayer, Jere and Jack Smith, Carol and Glen
Zumwalt*

While Dave was the first Yankee, Jack's arrival may
have been more of a shock to the family. Jack was a graduate
of Texas A&M, and, therefore, the first real Aggie in the
family. Charles attended Texas A&M for a short time but was
widely believed to have seen the error in his ways when he
transferred to University of Texas. University of Texas and
Texas A&M's storied rivalry required the Cyrus's to tap into
their deepest Christian graces in welcoming Jack.

As the Cyrus sisters each married and began to have
children, the family ties remained strong and visits were

frequent.

Figure 35 Back row: Janis, Glen, and Carol Zumwalt, Jere Smith, Shirley, Dave and Steve Mayer, Middle row: Marylee Zumwalt, Charles Smith, Charles and Vivian Cyrus holding Jennifer Smith, Pam Mayer, Front row: Paul and Alan Zumwalt, Peter, Mark and John Mayer (1970)

Charles and Vivian were committed, church-going Christians. They often attended University Baptist Church in Austin. It was their first church home when they came to Austin for summer school in 1927. Carol and Shirley grew up in this church and were married in the sanctuary

Vivian began working in library science when Jere was in high school and continued until 1971. She enjoyed helping the predominantly bi-lingual Mexican children attending Palm Elementary School to find books that interested them.

Upon retirement she had time to volunteer at Holy Cross Hospital coffee shop for 15 years and also to deliver Meals-on-Wheels during those years.

Charles retired from University of Texas in 1969 at the age of 70. He endeared himself to almost every librarian in Austin and later in Dickinson with his lost art of mending books.

Charles passed away July 19, 1989 in Dickinson, Texas. Vivian passed away November 2, 1990.

Charles and Vivian would be delighted to see all the new additions to the family since they married on that sunny day in June in 1927. The strong emphasis they placed on education, faith, service, and family is a heritage that has shaped the lives of their descendants in incalculable ways.

No individual or family springs into being without antecedents. Knowing the people and the stories that shaped our family history can offer wisdom and insight into how we choose to live and the legacy we'd like to leave for those who follow.

Appendix

Marriage Certificate for Louis Capt and Elizabeth Bratton

(Travis County Clerk's Office; Austin, Texas; Travis County Marriage Records; The Book Series: 1)

Land Grant for Louis Capt

"This is to certify that Lewis Capt is unconditionally entitled to three hundred and twenty acres of land as appeared by conditional certificate issued by the Board of Land Commissioners for Travis County hearing date, the 5th of April 1861. He having also proven to us that he has been an actual citizen of the Republic for the term of three years and that he has done and performed the duties required of him as such. Given under our hand and seal of the County this the 3rd day November 1845."

Louis Capt Obituary

"Louis Capt," Obituary; photocopy of newspaper clipping (source unknown), supplied October 8, 1991 by Clarice Childers Moore in a letter to Carol and Glen Zumwalt.

Died,—At the residence of his son, J. R. Capt, in Gonzales, Texas, on Friday, May 7, 1897, at 4:30 o'clock p. m. Louis Capt, aged 82 years, 10 months and 3 days.

Louis Capt was born in Geneva, Switzerland, on July 4, 1814. After traveling extensively over Europe he came to America in 1835 and lived for sometime in New York and New Jersey. He came to Galveston, Texas, in 1838 and lived there a few months, afterward moving to Austin where he remained until 1864. In 1842 he was united in marriage to Miss Elizabeth Bratton. They resided at Blanco, Texas, raising a family of two daughters and four sons. During Mr. Capt's early life in Texas he was identified with the stirring times, and spent a considerable time with "Big Foot" Wallace, fighting the Indians back and the struggle for Texas independence. About six months ago he moved from Blanco to Gonzales to reside with his son J. R. Capt. Like all old Texans Mr. Capt was kind and generous in heart and his name a pledge of honesty. His remains were interred in the Public cemetery Saturday evening.

The Scales Slaves

Dr. John Ball married Addie Pinck Scales just after the Civil War. The Scales family was a wealthy family with large plantations in North Carolina, Mississippi and Louisiana. Addie's great grandfather Colonel Nathaniel Scales gave each of his children a plantation and 10 slaves. Nathaniel and his children owned more than 2000 acres across four counties. Remnants of three plantations still stand: Mulburry Island, Deep Springs and High Rock Farm.

Robert Henry Scales was only 19 when his father Colonel Nathaniel Scales died in 1824. Robert Henry Scales was given "many acres between Reidsville and Yanceyville" in North Carolina. Their main crop was tobacco, which is extremely labor intensive. The labor was almost exclusively done by slaves. By 1860, the Federal Census tells us Robert Henry Scales had 52 slaves. Robert's son, William Nathaniel Scales, married Martha Jane Kaigler who inherited slaves from her plantation-owning family. Given the size of the Scales family, there were hundreds of slaves that worked the Scales' plantations.

The modern-day result is many African Americans with the last name Scales. It was common for slaves to take the surnames of their slave holders. In December 2018 I was contacted by an African American woman with the last name Scales who was genetically matched by Ancestry DNA to one of Charles Cyrus's daughters. Ancestry estimated the connection to be a 4th -6th cousins.

At this point, DNA tests cannot tell you HOW you are related, only how much common DNA you share with someone. Since there is some randomization in how DNA is passed along, it is not possible to know with certainty which generation connects the African American and white Scales' families but based on the amount of shared DNA, the connection is likely prior to the Civil War generation.

Even if there were no genetic connection between the families, the institution of slavery has inextricably linked African American Scales descendants and the white Cyrus/Scales descendants.

While attending a national genealogy conference in 2019, I met African American genealogists who explained the unique challenges of African American genealogy research. African Americans were not given the dignity of official documents such as birth, marriage and death certificates – which are the building blocks genealogical research. This means that many African Americans can only trace their family back a couple of generations before they hit what Dr. Louis Gates refers to as "the brick wall of slavery". One resource African American researchers look for are family papers -- such as plantation records – which slave holding families often retain because they are unaware of their importance or are too embarrassed to share.

I don't know if any extended relatives have any family papers or plantation records that might be of service to African American Scales genealogists, but I am happy to help disseminate any paperwork that might be helpful. Openly sharing whatever documentation, we have from the Scales' family records may be a resource for the African American Scales' families.

This brings me to Aunt Catherine. Catherine Scales was born into slavery in North Carolina around 1855. The title "Aunt" is honorific in that younger white people in the South referred to older black men and women as Aunt or Uncle. Her father was a slave of Nathaniel Scales (presumably Colonel Nathaniel Scales who lived 1756 – 1824, but it might be one of his sons). Between 1936 and 1938, the WPA hired writers to transcribe the stories of former slaves. This resulted in 17 volumes of slave narratives from all over the country. They are now online at The Library of Congress website

(https://www.loc.gov/collections/slave-narratives-from-the-federal-writers-project-1936-to-1938/about-this-collection/)
They interviewed three slaves in North Carolina with the last name Scales: Catherine Scales, Porter Scales, and Anderson Scales. Based on where they lived and their surname, their family lines all likely intersected (by "ownership" if not biology) with the extended family of our ancestor Colonel William Nathaniel Scales. I am including the Biography of Ex Slave Catherine Scales here because her poignant first-person account has stayed with me since I read it in 2016. Much like listening to someone's spiritual testimony, reading about Catherine's experiences as a slave is not a theoretical discussion of the topic of slavery but the lived experience of a real person.

The WPA transcribers attempted to record these stories in the African American dialect of the south in the 1930's. This can make some portions difficult to decode. I didn't want to directly edit the interview because after all these years, Catherine deserves to be heard in her own voice. However, I do offer a modernized paraphrase for those that find the original challenging.

Catherine's account of slavery sheds light on an aspect of Scales family history that is difficult to assimilate into the family narrative. I have also had to grapple with slave holders in my Virginia-based family tree. All we can do is learn from our ancestor's mistakes and try to make a positive contribution moving forward.

We may yet be contacted by more African American Scales descendants as DNA testing continues to grow in popularity. My hope in including Catherine's story, we can be better prepared to respond with understanding and empathy.

Biography of Ex-slave Catherine Scales
[Interviewed] by Miss Nancy Watkins
Madison, North Carolina
Rockingham County

About ten years old at the "Srenduh", now quite feeble, but aristocratic in her black dress, white apron and small sailor hat made of black taffeta silk with a milliner's fold around the edge, Aunt Catherine is small, intensely black with finely cut features and thin lip. Her hand is finely molded, fingers long and slender, Her voice is soft and poise marks her personality. Sallie Martin, a ginger cake colored woman, sixty-five, has lived as a kind of caretaker with Aunt Catherine since 1934 and thereby gets her own roof and refreshment. For Aunt Catherine has gotten "relief" from the county welfare chief, Mrs. John Lee Wilson, and Jeff Scales, seventy, brings Sallie to the "relief" dispensary in his two horse wagon for the apples or onions or grape fruits or prunes with dried bena, milk, canned beef or potatoes as the stores yield. A white horse and a brown mule comprise the team, and several dogs trot alongside. Sally also small and frail looking sits in a chair planted in the flat wagon bed behind the drivers' seat, a plank resting on the sides. Jeff drives close to the door, alights and helps Sallie step on to the back of the bed, thence to a chair he has placed, then to the ground, just as polite whites did to their women folks after the war when they would ride to town or to church or to picnics, in wagons in order to carry the family, the servants, the dinner, horse feed, water bucket, chairs, cushions. Sallie gets in line, presents Aunt Katherine's card, which she has gotten by mail, hears the dispensing lady call to the helping men what Aunt Catherine is to have, and struggles to the door with it where Jeff meets her, transfers the load to his wagon bed. Then with his hands he steadies Sallie as she mounts the chair, then the back of the wagon bed, over the side with voluminous long skirts, and old fashioned, ruffled sun bonnet. Off to the hilly north part of Madison called Freetown, Jeff's expertly guides his team through automobile traffic. During the worst of the depression Aunt Sallie said she kept her coal reserve in a tub upstairs so nobody could steal it.

Aunt Katherine strengthened by her relief food can talk comfortably.

"I shure did love my white fokes - Ole Marse, Timberlikk (Timberlake) an. Ole Miss Mary Timberlikk. My mother, Lucy Ann Timberlikk bough their portraits at the sale of the old Timberlake things, and kepp them an brought them with her to Madison, when we moved up here, an kepp them until mummy was in her last sickness, an' two of Ole Misses daughters came over from Greensboro, an' begged, - an mammy sold the pictures to them for a quarter a piece. I still have Ole Misses mother's dish, though. I've got in packed away in a safe place. I'll get it and show it to you. It is a large flat platter of the ware called iron ware and was generally used to serve fried ham and eggs while the gravy came in a small deep dish. In summer, a heap of snaps greasy with middling meat slashed and boiled down dry with Irish potatoes around the edge came to table in the platter.

The keeper of the Timberlake oil portraits was Lucy, slave of Nat Scales, and Lucy's husband was Nathan Scales. Slave Nat Scales (named for Marse Nat) had married a black woman who came 'across the water', Sallis Green who become by purchase Sallie Scales. Thus Aunt Katherine recalls her grandmother as one who 'cum over the water with a white lady'. The purchaser Mrs. Scales was from the LeSeur family. Her father was clerk of the Rockingham county court as early as and kept the

session records of his Presbyterian church in a fine neat
script.
"The LeSeurs had as big a house as the Scales house at
Deep Springs. I've stayed many a nite in it. It was next to
Ole Marse Jimmie Scaleses. John Durham Scales, Marse
Jimmy's grandson lived and died in it - his grandmother's
house, the old Le Seur place, ten miles down the Dan
river towards Leaksville, Miss Mary Le Seur married
Marse Gus Timberlikk, an was the grandmother of
William Timberlake Lipscomb who used to come up to
Madison and go to Dr. Schuck's Beulah Academy just
after the Srenduh. When Marse Billy'd get lonesome, he'd
go down to Spring Garden and dance with the
Scales girls. Ole Marse Le Seur is wife was Miss Lizzie
Scales Marse Jimmie's.

Nome, us slaves didn't have no chuch. Marse
Nat Scales ud let his slaves go to the babtizings.

I could hoe but I didn't do much clean-up
work. I spun on a great big wheel that we t m-1-1-11-. I
wish I had a big wheel to spin on right now. My
mammy, Lucy Ann, could weave. She sho loved her
white fokes. Cullud fokes didn't have much sence den.
She would take cow hair and kyard and spin it with a
little cottin into rolls, and then she'd weave cloth out of
it.

" An how they made their shoes den: My
father would cut shoes out of the raw cowhide and put
them on bottoms (soles) he cut out uv wood. An he
couldn't run in them a-tall, just had to stomp along! An
day didn't put on shoe till nearly Christmas.

Schooling
"Aunt Katherine said she 'learned her letters' in a
school fuh cullud fokes only taught by Mr. Sam Allen
just after the Srenduh close to the old Timber lake
place. Mr. Sam was the son of Mr. Val (entine) Allen an

Miss Betsy Martin (she was the granddaughter of
Governor Martin)
"Sometimes Miss Betsy'd git worried with
little nigguh rolling roun on de floor thub hader under
her feet, an' she'd say: "Gway! Gway!! Gway fum hyuh!
Gway tuh Pamlico! An the little nigguhsia say: 'Miss
Betsy, whah's Pamplico?'
'Nine miles tother sede of hell!
      "Yesin Mr. Sam Allen learn't me my letters.
He was crippled. He married a Grogan, an' two Allen
girls married Grogans - one, Mary! Mr. Val's father was
William Allen. I went to Mr. Vaul Allen's funeral an he
was buried on his father's ole place, an Miss Betsy too.
      "How de cullud fokes did hate to be sold
down south in de cotton country! One time ole Marse
Jimmy Scales wuz go sell uh hunduhd down south, and
he died, an all de cullud fokes wuz glad he died cause he
wuz go sell um, an oftuh he died, day didn!t halftuh be
sold way fum home.
      "One slave woman wuz sold way fum home -
had three chillun, and daze six an eight an ten yuhs ole.
She sang a song juss fo day tuh hub off. She put her three
children between her knees. She sung, Lord, Be With
Us. "
      [Aunt Katherine sings:] "Remembuh me,
Remembuh me, Oh Lord, remembuh me" This was sung
full of quavers and pathos, and entreaty.
      "Den she cried! An dey took huh off, and de
chillun never saw her no more.
      "Aftuh I learned my lettuhs at Marse Sam Al
lens school, I learned a Bible verse ebry day an if I want
bixxy I'd learn ah half uh chaptuh. I read some
newspapers, and some story books de Miss Mary
Timberlikk gave us chillun to read an look ovuh. I
learned to write in a copy book, an I'd write stories

about Christ, and several different stories. I filled a great
big copy book with practice. I learned the most, tho',
from Webstuh's Weekly in Reidsville. We took that
papuh goin on five yuhs. I read evrything in it.
        "Nome, I didn't know Miss Irene McGehiet.
Uncle John R. Webster made that paper. It sure wuz a
good paper!

My daddy wuz Marse Nat's slave, an Porter Scales waz
his slave too. Ole Marse Jimmie Scale's sons was Nat
Pitcher and John Durham, and John Durham went to
wah. He took Richmond Scales long with him to wait
on him! Cook fuh him! Make his pallet! Clean his
clothes! Rub down his horse! Marse John Durum sleep
with Richmond in de wintuh to keep him warm.
Richmond'd carry him watuh in his canteen during a
battle. Marse John Durum had on a ring that wuz
carved and he tole Richmond take a good look at this
ring sose he'd know him by it, if he didn't kum up aftuh
a battle. Richmond ud hole onto his hawse's tail, an go
wif him fuhs he could fo a battle.
        "Yes'm I [married], Richmond Scales when he
wuz a widower an had a boy named Jeff. I never had no
chillun. Jeff's (70) seventy now, an lives right ovuh cross
de street dere in the other hous the Vadens built sixty
years ago. I live in one, too."
        Aunt Katherine's house has a front room
with stairway in the corner leading to one above. A back
door leads to a side porch flanked by a two roomed ell,
and ended by a pantry. Chimneys with fireplaces once
gave heat, but economy had put in Aunt Katherine's tiny
stove which she a lump at a time in the winters of de
pression and relief 1932 - 1937.

A big fat clean double bed, bureau, wash stand, "centuh"table, chairs and the stairway con sumed the living room floor space.

"Nome! I joined de chuch after a big meet in held by preacher Richard Walker about 1907. I joined the Methodist Chuch an I have always loved to go tuh chuch. This street goes on and goes into the Mayodan road at our new brick (1925) Methodist Chuch. Richmond Scales, my husband died long ago; my mother, about four years ago. She was very old! I wanted to move to Reidsville when we leff de ole plantation whab we could get more wok (waiting) waten on wimmen (obstetries) but the men fokes had kin fokes up hyuh, an we keem hyuh.

"I know whah de ole Sharp graveyard 'bout two miles fum (east) Madison close to Mist Tunnuh (Turner) Peay's; cause lots uh cullud fokes buried there an I went to the funerals. I could go straight tuh it.

Modernized paraphrase by Carla Whitacre Mayer

Author's Note: *Catherine Scales is interviewed sometime between 1937-1938 by a Miss Nancy Watkins in Catherine's home in Rockingham, North Carolina.*

I found the list of questions WPA interviewers were supposed to ask and have included the questions where they seem to fit.

Introduction by Miss Nancy Watkins:

Catherine Scales was 10 years old when the Civil War ended. She is now quite feeble, but aristocratic in her black dress, white apron and small sailor hat made of black taffeta sick with a milliner's fold around the edge. Catherine is small, intensely black with finely cut features and thin lip. Her hand is finely molded, fingers long and slender. Her voice is soft, and poise marks her personality.

Catherine's caretaker, Sallie Martin, has worked for Catherine in exchange for room and board since 1934. Sallie is a ginger-cake colored woman of 65.

Sallie is driven by Catherine's stepson, Jeff Scales, to the Welfare food dispensary in a wagon pulled by a white horse and a brown mule. Sallie looks small and frail sitting in a chair on the back of the flat-bed wagon.

When Jeff arrives, he helps Sallie out of the wagon and sets her chair on the ground, just like polite whites did for women after the war when they rode to town for church and picnics, carrying family, servants, food, horse feed, water buckets, chairs and cushions.

Sallie gets in line and presents Catherine's Welfare card, which she received in the mail, and the Welfare lady calls out what Catherine is allowed to have from the food stores.

Sallie struggles to the door with her load and Jeff meets her to transfer the load to his wagon bed. Sallie now steps on her chair in her voluminous long skirts and old-fashioned ruffled sun bonnet and climbs back into the wagon.

They drive to the hilly north part of Madison called Freetown as Jeff expertly guides his team through automobile traffic. Sallie mentions that during the worst of the Depression, she kept her coal reserve in a tub upstairs so nobody could steal it.

Once Catherine sees her food stores delivered, she is ready to sit down and be interviewed.

Catherine's Interview:

Presumed Question: Tell us about your master, mistress, their children, and the house they lived in.

" I sure did love my white folks – Old Master Timberlake and Miss Mary Timberlake. My mother, Lucy Ann Timberlake bought their portraits at a sale of old Timberlake things and brought them to Madison when we moved here. She kept them almost to the end of her life when two of Mary Timberlake daughters came from Greensboro and begged to buy them. My mother sold them the pictures for a quarter a piece.

I still have a dish that belonged to Mary Timberlake's mother. I've packed it away in a safe place. I'll get it and show it to you. It is a large flat iron platter called ironware and generally used to serve friend ham and eggs, while the gravy came in a small deep dish. In summer, a heap of [sugar]snaps -- greasy with middling meat slashed and boiled down dry with Irish potatoes -- sat around the edge of the platter.

The keeper of the Timberlake oil portraits was a slave to Nat Scales. Her husband was Nathan Scales, named after

Master Nat. He married a black woman named Sallie that "come over the water with a white lady." The white lady was Mrs. Scales, whose maiden name was LeSeur. Her father was the clerk of Rockingham County Court as early as we kept session records of his Presbyterian church in fine neat script.

The LeSeurs had a big house next to Master Jimmy Scales' house on the Deep Springs Plantation[1] I've stayed in the LeSeur's house many a night. John Durham Scales, Master Jimmy's grandson, lived and died in the old LeSeur place. It's 10 miles down the Dan River towards Leaksville.

Miss Mary LeSeur married Master Gus Timberlake Lipscomb who used to come up to Madison to go to Dr. Schuck's Beula Academy just after the war. When Master Billy would get lonesome, he'd go down to Spring Garden and dance with the Scales girls. Old Master Le Seur's wife was Lizzie Scales, Master Jimmy's daughter.

Presumed question: Did the slaves have a church on your plantation?

No, we didn't have a church. Master Nat Scales would let his slaves go to baptisms.

Presumed question: Tell what work you did and how you lived the first year after the war.

I could hoe, but I didn't do much clean-up work. I spun on a great big wheel that went "m-m-m-m-m". I wish I had a big wheel to spin on right now. My mother, Lucy Ann, could weave. She sure loved her white folks. Colored folks didn't have much sense then. She would take cow hair and

---

[1] We know that James Madison Scales, brother of our direct descendant Robert Henry Scales, was bequeathed Deep Springs Plantation.

she would card and spin it with a little cotton into rolls and then she'd weave cloth out of it.

My father made shoes by cutting out the raw cowhide and making soles out of wood. You couldn't run in them at all, you just had to stomp along! So, they didn't put shoes on until nearly Christmas.

Presumed question: Did the white folks help you to learn to read and write?

Interviewer paraphrases Catherine: Catherine said she "learned her letters' after the war in a school for colored folks taught by Mr. Sam Allen. It was located by the old Timberlake place. Mr. Sam was the son of Mr. Valentine Allen and Miss Betsy Martin (she was the granddaughter of Governor Martin).[xlvi]

Quoting Catherine directly: Sometimes Miss Betsy would be bothered by colored kids rolling around on the floor under feet and she'd say, 'Go away! Go away! Go away from here. Go to Pamlico!' And the kids would ask 'Miss Betsy what's Pamlico?' She'd say, 'Nine miles on the other side of hell!'

Yes, Mr. Sam Allen taught me my letters. He was crippled. He married a Grogan and two Allen girls married Grogans....Mr. Val's father was William Allen. I went to Mr. Valentine Allen's funeral and he was buried on his father's old place, and so was Miss Betsy.

Presumed question: Did you ever see any slaves sold or auctioned off?

How colored folks hated being sold down south in cotton country! One time, old Master Jimmy Scales was going to sell a hundred slaves down south but he died before the sale. All the colored folks were glad he died because after his death they didn't have to be sold away from home.

[I saw] one woman who was sold away from home. She had three children and they were 6,8, and 10 years old. She put them between her knees and sang them a song. She sang. "Lord , Be With Us."

[Catherine sings the song] Remember me, Remember me, Oh Lord, remember me. [The interviewer notes] This was sung full of quavers and pathos and entreaty.

[Catherine quoted directly] Then the mother cried! And they took her off and she never saw her children again.

Presumed question: Did slaves read the Bible?

After I learned my letters at Master Sam Allen's school, I learned a Bible verse every day and if I wanted a cookie, I'd learn half a chapter. I read some newspapers and some storybooks that Miss Mary Timberlake gave her children to read. I learned to write in a copy book. And I'd write stories about Christ, and lots of other things. I learned the most, though, from Webster's Weekly in Reidsville. We got the paper for five years and I read everything in it....It sure was a good paper!

Presumed Question: What do you remember about the war that brought your freedom?

My daddy was Master Nat's slave – and Porter Scales was his slave, too. Old Master Jimmie Scales's sons was Nat Pitcher and John Durham. When John Durham went to war, he took my husband Richmond Scales to war to wait on him! He cooked for him, made up his bed, cleaned his clothes, and rubbed down his horses! Master John Durham would sleep with Richmond in the winter to keep warm. Richmond would carry water in his canteen during a battle. Master John Durham had a carved ring he wore, and he told Richmond to take a good look at the ring, so he could use it to identify his body if he died in battle. Richmond would have to hold on to his horse's tail and go with him as far as he could go into battle.

I married Richmond Scales when he was a widower and had boy named Jeff. I never had children. Jeff is 70 now and lives right across the street there in the other house the Vandens build sixty years ago. I live in one, too.

[Interviewer comments] Catherine's house has a front room with a stairway in the corner leading upstairs. A back door leads to a side porch flanked by an L-shaped room that ends with a pantry. Chimneys with the fireplaces once gave heat, but Welfare gave Catherine a tiny stove during the Depression and now she burns one lump of coal at a time.

A big fat clean double bed, a bureau, washstand, center table, chairs and the stairway consume the living room floor place.

Presumed question: Did you have a favorite preacher?

[Quoting Catherine]: No. I joined the church after a big meeting held by preacher Richard Walker about 1907. I joined the Methodist Church and I have always loved to go to church. This street goes on and goes into Mayodan road at our new brick (1925) Methodist church. Richmond Scales, my husband died long ago; my mother, about four years ago. She was very old. I wanted to move to Reidsville when we left the old plantation so we get more work waiting on women (obstetrics) but the men folk had family up here and we came to Madison.

I know the old Sharp graveyard, it's about two miles east of Madison close to Miss Turner's place. A lot of colored folks are buried there, and I went to the funerals. I could go straight to it.

Record of John Ball's Civil War Service

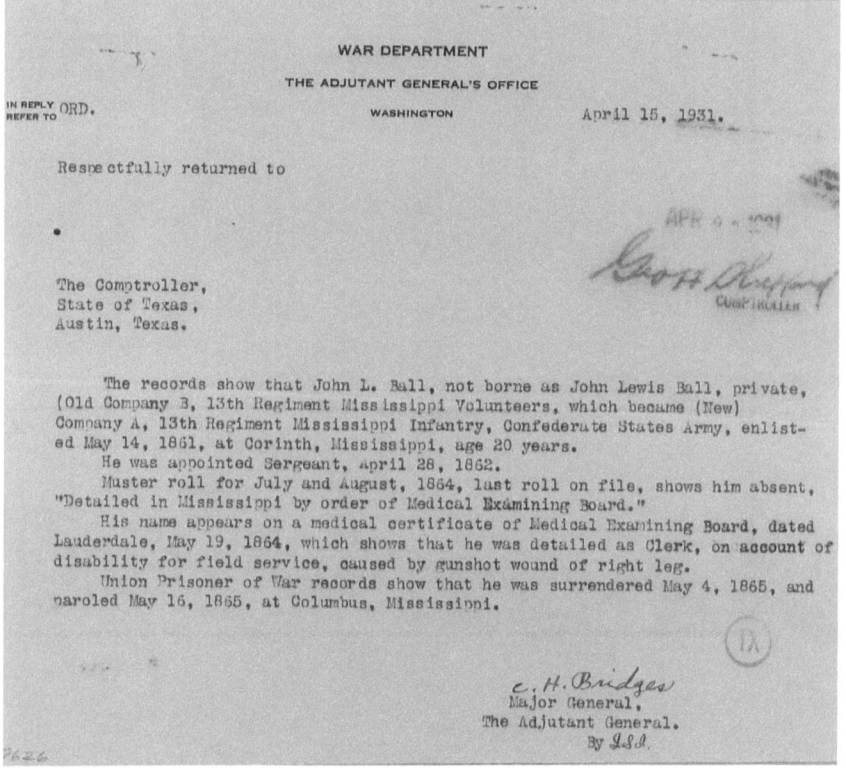

Government Summary of John Ball's Civil War Service

John Ball's Medical Discharge Certificate

John Ball's Obituary

The Winston County Journal (Louisville, Mississippi). 13 Mar
1936

WINSTON COUNTY JOURNAL
Will C. Hight _____ **Editor**

Entered at the Post Office at
Louisville, Miss., as matter
of the second class.

LETTER FROM DR. FOSTER

We are in receipt of a letter from Dr. John C. Foster, of Clarksville, Texas, in which he encloses notice of the death of Dr. John Ball. Since Dr. Foster's letter contains some old history which may be of interest to our older people, we reproduce it as follows:

Clarksville, Texas, March 8.
Mr. W. C. Hight,
Louisville, Miss.
Dear Friend:

I am today sending you a copy of the Dallas sJournal containing a notice of the death of Dr. John L. Ball, a native of Winston and a long time ago lived in Louisville and clerked for my father, Dr. Edward Foster. John Ball left Louisville a member of the Winston Guards, John Bradley, Captain. Before leaving the company 125 strong was assembled in front of an old brick building near the Hotel I think run by Mrs. Jeff Hughes where Miss Lou Covington made a speech, presenting the company a flag. Miss Covington was one of the prettiest girls, and one of the brightest of Louisville. She afterwards married Jim Hughes, son of Jeff Hughes. The company stood assembled to bid good bye to friends and relatives whose eyes were streaming with tears and the girls bestowing kisses at random. Mr. Nick Pyle seeing his opportunity tanked up on Pink Cooper's bottle was running wild crying like a freshly spanked baby and kissing all the pretty girls, but none of the old women, was having the time of his life. I was standing near Col. Wm. Bolling near where Wrag's store on the south side of the street. Bolling says "John, who is that fellow." I told him "Nick Pyle." Bolling said

"By G— the worst case of piles I ever saw." Nick was not a member of the company. Jasper, a brother of John Ball, lost a leg. John and Jasper were both members of Bradley's Company and cousins to Tom Patty. All three of the Bradleys were killed.

Your friend,
JOHN C. FOSTER.

____

FUNERAL FOR DR. J. L. BALL AT CLEBURNE

Vet of Civil War, Long Resident of Texas, Succumbs at 95.

Cleburne, Texas, March 7. — Dr. J. L. Ball, 95, died at a local sanitarium after an illness of several weeks. Funeral services were held Saturday morning at the first Baptist Church.

Dr. Ball was born in Mississippi. He fought in some of the hardest battles of the Civil War. Wounded at Gettysburg, he was held prisoner for some months, and after being exchanged he continued his service to the South in the Quartermaster's Department. Immediately after the war he resumed his medical studies and after his graduation went to Greenwood, Miss., where he began his practice of medicine. He came to Texas in 1872, first settling in Calvert, but came to Johnson County in 1876 and had been a resident of Cleburne since 1907.

Surviving are seven children.

____○____

DEATH OF UNCLE JEFF MITCHELL

On Thursday night February 13, 1936, God sent His angel down and carried away Uncle Jeff Mitchell (colored), who was then 82 years old. He was born and reared in Winston county where he spent his entire life.

He joined Rock Port M. E. church when quite young and lived a consistent Christian life, during which time he served in many capacities, and was a class leader from the time of his initiation in the church until his death.

What I Know and Remember About My Father Charles Lewis Cyrus
by Addie Scales Cyrus (Doll)

Charles Lewis Cyrus was born September 12, 1870 in Maury County, Tennessee. He was the first of eight children born to Charles Volney and Anna Maria Cyrus. He had four brothers and three sisters. His father was a farmer.

Charles Lewis and his brother Jim, one year younger, came to Cleburne, Texas circa 1890. He bought some acreage on North Buffalo Street and they began building a house to be the home of their parents and siblings. When the house was finished, and the family settled, Charles Lewis started a business handling feed, grain, and coal which he bought by the train-car load. It was a prosperous undertaking.

I know none of the particulars of how or when he and my mother Jennie Lewis Ball became aware of each other. It may have been in 1893 because that was the year she had graduated from Baylor University and had been selected as the young lady to represent Johnson County at the World's Fair being held in Chicago that summer. Her older brother, William (called Buddy) had also finished Baylor that year and accompanied her on this exciting trip. It was a wonderful memory for her. She often spoke of it as I was growing up.

After her return from Chicago she taught for several years in schools near her home. There must have been a

romance because he (Charles Lewis Cyrus) began and
finished a house for them to move into after their marriage
on June 15, 1898. I have no knowledge of this wedding
either, but I remember seeing her wedding dress which was
among other interesting things she kept in her large trunk
that had gone to Baylor with her.

This house must have been his dream home because
he put so many "extras" into it. It was a one and a half story
gingerbread trimmed Victorian style dwelling on a corner lot
facing south extending from Featherstone Street to College
Street on the north side. The lot may have been seventy-five
feet or more and it seemed wide. The location was near the
city limits on the westside of Cleburne. There were no
houses in front for quite a distance and none at all on the
west side of our house until most of us were grown-up. But
across the streets on the east and north, and on and on and
on were neighbors. This open space added much enjoyment

to us through the years. Dad had chosen a wonderful location for his future family. I think he put much of himself into the house he built for his bride. It was also a dream house to me for my years there were happy times.

Among the "extras" he put in were two stained-glass windows, one small one over the large plate glass window placed at the center of a bay window in the front extension of the house. The larger oval shaped stained-glass window was on the east side of the entrance hall overlooking that side of the rounded front porch.

Another "extra" was a built-in drainboard in the kitchen. It was made of wood with grooves to guide the drain-water back into the sink. Each groove was lined with a narrow strip of wood to support the dishes while they drained.

The most elaborate "extra" to me was the built-in china-closet in the wainscoted dining room. The china closet extended from near the ceiling to near the floor. The upper part was enclosed by two glass doors behind which were shelves for dishes. The wedding presents were on the upper shelves and our everyday dishes on the bottom one. Beneath this part were two long and two narrow drawers which held table linens and silver-ware. Above the two narrow drawers was a narrow mirror extending on up to near the ceiling. To the right of this mirror and drawers the china closet curved back into the north wall near to the door leading to the kitchen. The shelves extended into this curved area, but not the drawers.

I think of my father as a handsome man. He had black hair with a slight curl to it and brown eyes. He was circa 5'10" in height and of sturdy build, not fat. He was especially handsome on Sunday, when he dressed to go to church, in his white shirt, tie, and dark suit. I especially liked his Sunday shoes with a patent leather toe. In the early days we went as a family to the Main Street Methodist Church of which he was a Charter Member, having joined it when he first came to Cleburne. He remained a member and attended this church regularly, throughout his life.

I do not know when or why the feeling of animosity developed between my parents. I never saw any expression or sign of affection between them. At best, they were civil toward each other. But remember, I was their fourth child; they had endured a long siege of typhoid fever which almost killed Dad, while mom was pregnant with me. By the time I was old enough to be conscious of their relationship Dad had lost his business and was now trying to make a living by farming. The returns of which never seemed to be enough - although I didn't know this until later. Mom was now teaching elocution and physical culture to young girls who came to our house for their lessons. One girl did sewing for us in exchange for my mother's lessons. Sis and I were in on these lessons too!

Back to their relationship: I think Grandma Ball as well as the Cyrus family were responsible for much of their trouble. From the beginning Grandma Ball did not like Charlie Cyrus, I don't know why, but it could have been that he was not a college man. Grandma and her two sisters had graduated from Columbia Athenaeum in Tennessee and Grandpa was a graduate of Medical school. Mom and her brothers were college graduates. She naturally thought, I suppose, that Mom could "do better". From my viewpoint:

I can understand that Mom was flattered that a handsome, as well as prosperous, young man wanted to marry her. Mom was not a physically pretty woman - her teeth were too large. (She looked 100% better after getting false teeth). She had had "no luck" with college men while she was in college- so why not marry this "hometown boy"? Now Grandma's final attempt to prevent this marriage was to tell Mom, "If you marry Charlie Cyrus, I will never enter your house." Mom did and Grandma stuck to her threat. (I never knew of Dad being in Grandma's house, either). Another angle for her disapproval may have been that she didn't want her only daughter to marry anybody!

The Cyrus family angle of their marital problems, that I was told, was the practice of Dad's three single sisters charging their purchases of pretty clothes to dad's account. Mom wanted him to stop this, but he never did.

This may be a good place to mention that Dad told Mom (at what junction in their life together, it was not revealed) that he was in love with and wanted to marry his sweetheart he left in Tennessee, but because she had an insane relative he changed his mind because he didn't want his children to inherit this strain. How many times he may have reminded her that his sweetheart was in Tennessee we are not told.

In addition to family interference, each of my parents was a strong individual. This characteristic caused much friction between them. One time that their wills crossed concerned the punishment of my brother Charles, their first-born child. The offense for which my father intended to discipline him has not been handed down; the manner and implement has been. He meant to whip him with a switch. I do not know the age of my brother on this occasion, but my mother was so concerned, she interfered because (as she described the scene later) the switch was a tree-limb which would have resulted in the child being beaten. Her interference prevented the punishment and rankled my father. It was a sore spot between them forever after. There is no account of any further punishment administered by him, but plenty of times my mother spanked me, John, and Ralph always at the same time, one after the other, each observing the other two "getting it". If my mother or father ever administered physical punishment to Sis or Charles, I never heard of it. Neither did our father ever whip me or John or Ralph to my knowledge. He was not abusive with my mother, except orally.

My memory of Dad is sad rather than bad. I think he was a good man morally and physically. He worked hard (without making much money). He did not drink liquor of any kind; he did not use tobacco; he did not "chase the women," he did not remarry after the divorce. He was steady in his habits. I knew him as a farmer. The back half of our homeplace was the barn lot. There was a barn, a cow, chickens, and three horses. We also had pigs kept a short distance from our house, outside the city limits. We could see them and hear the noise from our yard. When butchered, the meat was cured in the smokehouse in our backyard. Dad attended to all that.

Dad went to the farm each day in the wagon. Often Ralph and I would run to meet him in the afternoon. He'd stop for us to climb up and ride on home part of the way with him. He had us, with John, shucking corn to have ready to feed the stock.

Often, we hand-ground some of the corn, after shelling it, for chicken feed. We also had to pick peanuts from the hay which Dad had brought in from the farm. The peanuts went to the house, the hay was stock feed. Dad allowed us to ride the horses when they were not being used. Dot and Dixie were very gentle, but Hai, a stallion, was off limits to us. I never saw my brother Charles on a horse, but Sis, John, Ralph and I had many happy hours on them. We rode in our front yard at first and later on the open prairie in front of the house - most always bareback.

I have wondered what effect the names of us kids had on the relationships. My brother Charles was given Grandpa Cyrus' full name: Charles Volney Cyrus which he never liked and had Volney dropped, legally, when he came of age. Sis got Mom's full name: Jennie Lewis; the next child, John William, was the name of Mom's father and two of her brothers with no connection to Dad's side. Then the second daughter was given Grandma Ball's full name: Addie Scales. My youngest brother became Ralph Lynn, with no family connection at all-- except that Lynn is the name of the West Texas County in which Dad had some property which was sold during his typhoid illness.

I got the idea from several of their arguments that Dad blamed Mom for selling his property. It also occurred to me that Buddy was the purchaser. Without knowing for sure, I also thought that on occasion Mom had received money from Buddy in time of need. Anyway, the sale of this property was a sore spot between them. It was part of and a continuation of an earlier disagreement in which Dad had wanted to leave Cleburne and get established on this West

Texas acreage. But Mom would not consider it. She absolutely refused.

Dad called Sis "Dinah" for a long time, but because she didn't like it he finally stopped. He called me "Dollikins" which was okay with me, and the family picked it up, but shortened it to Doll, which has continued to the present. I imagine there was discussion, and possibly disagreement, at the time [each of us was born].

It dawned on me one day that Dad was taking no part in family activity. He was not eating at the table with us and stayed in his own room. On one occasion when I was in his room, he was eating an apple. He offered to get me one, if I wanted it, and took it from a barrel full of apples which was in the corner behind his bed. This became the procedure followed every time. John and Ralph sometimes shared his generosity with me. If any of the others did, I didn't notice it. We never got any unless he got them for us when he was home. We ate while we sat and talked with him.

One day when I was eleven or so, I was informed that Mom had gotten a divorce and that Dad was leaving us. I was stunned and didn't know what to do or what to say. As I think of it now, I cry. I was never conscious of him moving any clothes or other possessions from the house.

It seemed so sudden. On this day we (and I am not sure who, but I was not alone), were standing on the front porch. Mom and Dad were in the yard just below us. They were both calm. We said, "Goodbye". He stood there a bit longer with no other words, then turned and walked away. There were no tears, no kisses…only silence. Nobody moved for several minutes, then slowly and quietly, we scattered.

He called once, not long after, and asked if he could come to see us. Mom said, "Yes." I remember we all sat quietly in the living room with very polite conversations. He didn't stay long. Another time, much later, he called and wanted to talk to Sis. She answered and held the phone while she relayed his message to Mom. He had been to the going-out-of- business sale of a jewelry store, and had bought a set of silverware and wanted to give it to Sis. Mom said for her to do what she wanted to about accepting it. She got back to him and said, "No, thank you". He then made the same offer to me and I gave him the same reply. I don't think I saw him again until after I married. John had been to see him and told us about him. He was with his parents in the home he had built for them on North Buffalo St. But he was busy building a rather small house on the lot next to them. He moved into it before it was finished, continued working to finish it and then sold it and started on a second one on the lot next to it: following the same pattern with this house and also a third one on the next lot.

For relaxation during this period he developed a garden behind each house and planted fruit trees. It provided some food as well as diversity for him. His parents had both died in the meantime. They are buried in the same cemetery and not far from the Ball plot.

Six or seven years had gone by without any contact between Dad and me. I realized I was lonesome for him. I had always known that I was his favorite child. My mother's influence was such that neither of us could really show our mutual affection. But when I married, I told C.P. that I wanted to see him He was really glad to see us and was enthusiastic in telling us of his activities and showing us his

garden. He was interested in hearing about us and our
interests.

From that time on, every time we were in Cleburne
we went by and visited with him for an hour or so. He
shared with us the garden produce he had on hand and
insisted that we take it. He assured us each time that he was
comfortable, healthy and contented with his situation. His
neighbors were friendly and often invited him to share a
meal with them. His bicycle was parked on the front porch
and he told us he rode it to Main Street Methodist Church
every Sunday.

Through the next few years we exchanged letters fairly
often. I don't think I saved any, though. In one letter he told
me his old sweetheart from Tennessee would be in
Cleburne to see him on such and such a date and wanted
her to meet me. C.P. and I made a special trip and had a
nice visit with them She was a nice-looking person with a
pleasing personality-even jolly. I understood how he could
have been attracted to her in earlier times. Babs was with us
as usual and made a good impression on the visit.

Dad had always been pleased to see his grandchild-
possibly the only one of his grandchildren he ever saw.
However, he didn't "take on over her". He was content with
adult conversation.

I don't remember the date of the last time I saw my
father. We had spent the weekend with Mom and Ralph and
left them in time to meet Dad as the Methodist morning
service ended. We parked and sat in the car until we saw
him walking down the steps. His two sisters from Corpus
Christi were with him, Aunt Susie and Aunt Roberts. We
had a congenial meeting there on the sidewalk. We invited

them to have lunch with us but they said they had reservations across the street at a private home that had a public dining room and asked us to join them. We did. This was familiar territory, because it was the old Wimberly home next door to Grandma Ball's house, which was still there. Other people from church were at the long table; the food was being served family-style. We were introduced to the people near us. One of them I had already recognized and spoken to. He was Dr. Gerstenkorn, a dentist, who had worked on my teeth not too many years before. He recognized me too. We visited while we ate but did not tarry long afterwards. It was the first time I had seen my aunts for years. They planned to go back to Corpus Christi that afternoon, and we were anxious to get on our way too. So we parted with good wishes all around.

The next news I had about Dad was from Buddy. He told us that Dad's two sisters had placed him in the State Institution in Terrell, Texas. Buddy had been Dad's doctor all through the years. He communicated to us a bit later that he had been to Terrell to check on Dad. He was pleased to report that Dad was doing well; he seemed to be contented in his new surroundings. The officials at the Institution told Buddy that Dad was well adjusted and was friendly with his associates and was always happy to oblige when called on to ask the blessing before meals.

Not long after this report Buddy sent me a clipping from the Cleburne paper stating that Charles Lewis Cyrus had died on Oct. 14. 1960 in Terrell, Texas and was buried in Cleburne, Texas. His life spanned ninety years and one month and two days. Mom lived to be eighty-six years and a few months. Her death occurred on Feb. 6, 1959.

Dad is buried on the cemetery plot with his parents and the infant baby of Uncle Jim and Aunt Lily. This plot is on the same drive and not far from the Ball plot where Mom and Pop are buried. Ralph and I promised each other we would erect a stone for Dad's grave with the same wording that's on Mom's, but with the correct dates for Dad's life span. We never got around to it. Now, I plan to arrange for it the next time I'm in Cleburne. Jere, you remind me if your plan materializes for the Fall trip to Cleburne. I was invited and accepted the invitation to act as guide after we get there.

Written by Addie Scales Cyrus (known as Doll)

History of the Dr. John Lewis Ball Family: Beginning September 15, 1840
by Empriss Jowell Ball May 1967

FOREWORD: This is a brief history of the lives of two Johnson County Pioneers, DR. JOHN LEWIS BALL and his wife ADDIE PINCK SCALES BALL, AND the SEVEN CHILDREN born to them. It would have been a satisfaction probably to all concerned, to have also listed occupations of members of this family, residence, etc. but this was not feasible.

Grateful expression of thanks is hereby made to the various members of the BALL FAMILY for their interest and aid in furnishing data during the writing of this article.

Compiled by Empriss Jowell Ball (wife of Robert L. Ball), with the final printing being done by Charles Cyrus of The University of Texas at Austin.

DR. JOHN LEWIS BALL,

One of a family of thirteen children, [John]was born in Louisville, Mississippi, September 15, 1840. His father, Francis Marion Ball, born 1913 in Abbeville County, South Carolina, migrated to Alabama, thence to Louisville, Mississippi, where he reared his family, moving in his old age to Greenville, Texas, where he and his wife died.

At the age of eighteen Dr. Ball started his medical education as a pharmacy clerk in a Louisville drugstore, studying medicine at night. After the Civil War, he went to

Louisville Kentucky Medical College, receiving his credentials there, then located in Greenwood, Mississippi, to practice his profession.

Dr. J. L. Ball volunteered with the Confederacy, serving with the Thirteenth Mississippi Regiment under the command of Col. William Barksdale. He participated in various battles: Battle of Manassas, Leesburg, Garner's Farm, Seven Pines, and Gettysburg where he was wounded July 3, 1863 when a bullet from an enemy gunshot blew away part of his knee cap. On July 4, he was taken prisoner and moved to Davis Island. Here in the hospital he spent four months as a prisoner patient, during which time the doctors decided it would be best to remove his leg. Dr. Ball opposed this very bitterly refusing to take an anesthetic while under treatment for fear they would remove it in spite of his wishes. He felt such a loss would be a detriment to him in his desire to practice medicine. Respect for his stamina and his wish to succeed in his profession, caused the decision by the doctors to forego the operation and to do everything in their power that was possible to help him toward recovery. He made good progress and was sent home to rest and recuperate. Finally, he was exchanged for a Northern soldier-prisoner, and spent the remainder of the Civil War in the Quartermaster's Department.

Dr. Ball was married Feb. 25, 1869 to MISS ADDIE PINCK SCALES at her plantation home on the Yazoo River near the town of Greenwood, Mississippi. The plantation is now owned by the wife and son of Mr. Leslie Scales, only brother of Mrs. Ball).

MRS. ADDIE PINCK SCALES BALL was born near Greenwood, Mississippi, May 23, 1851. One of three children born to Nathaniel Irving Scales and Martha Kaigler Scales, she was one of many in the Old South whose childhood was clouded by the tragedy of the Civil War. Her father was in the service of the United States Army when the South seceded. When Mississippi became one of the States of the Confederacy, he defected and fought with his home regiment. Captured early in the war, he was a prisoner of the North and assigned to nursing duties in Overton Military Hospital, Memphis, Tennessee, Jan. 1864. His last letter written to his pre-teen age daughter, Addie, cited the fact that small Pox was rampant in the hospital. Her mother was of German descent, born in Georgia, truly an aristocrat of the South, steeped in all of its traditions. She reared her three children, conducted affairs pertaining to the plantation, and lived a good life until she died at 83 years of age in 1908.

Mrs. A. P. Ball (her business signature) was educated in Columbia Athenaeum College, Columbia, Tennessee. She was married to Dr. J. L. Ball on February 25, 1869 when she was 17 years of age, prior to her eighteenth birthday on May 23rd. Her life was a testament to the saying about the women of the old South: They are like a sword -- they will bend and bend but never break." Reared in the lap of luxury, servants to do her bidding, yet she spent her mature life in hardships of the frontier that meant constant self-denial in order that her children could have an education and the best cultural opportunities.

SEVEN CHILDREN were born to this couple: The first-born was WILLIAM PINCK BALL, the only one of their children who was a native of Mississippi. In 1872 because of the prevalence of malaria in the "Delta Country", a decision was made to move to Texas. Two of Dr. Ball's brothers accompanied the young family to Calvert, Texas, operating a "country store there and Dr. Ball practicing medicine. Still plagued by yellow fever and malaria after four years in Calvert, Dr. and Mrs. Ball with their three children moved to a higher altitude, buying a farm in Johnson County in 1876. This farm home is located five miles north of what is now the town of Cleburne. At that time, it was only a village. Lumber and supplies for the home and farm had to be freighted from Fort Worth. After 31 years spent on the farm where all seven children were reared to adulthood, the final move was made by this aging couple to a new twelve-room home located at 411 North Main Street, Cleburne, Texas. There they spent the last sixteen years of their life together, Mrs. Ball preceding her husband in death on July 27, 1923, at 72 years of age.

Both Dr. J. L. Ball and his wife made a wonderful contribution to Johnson County. Gentle folk in the highest sense of the word, they supported educational, civic, social and religious units sponsoring the essence of all things cultural, participating in all features that were upbuilding in their community.

Letter from Charles Cyrus

Author's Note: *Charles Cyrus (age 84) and Ann Murphy (age 24) ran into one another at a University of Texas function in 1983. It's possible Ann was related to some old family friends, also named the Murphy's. Ann was just starting out as a teacher and Charles had spent his life "teaching teachers how to teach." He begins a long correspondence with her that seems to last until 1987. If I were title this collection, I would title it "Letters to Young Teacher". Below is an excerpt of one letter where Charles talks about his youth in Cleburne, Texas.*

Austin, Texas
September 18, 1983

Note to Ann Murphy in Cleburne, Texas-----GREETINGS
It was nice talking to you when you were in Austin, Texas, attending the anniversary celebration of The University of Texas. This little visit with you caused me to start thinking of events and situations that I am familiar with that happened before I left Cleburne in 1923 to enter the University of Texas as a Freshman.

Cleburne wasn't a one-horse town; there were many horses as horses were the means of transportation. My grandfather and grandmother, Dr. & Mrs. J. L. Ball, moved from the farm to town in 1908. They brought the milk cow and their horse and buggy. They used the horse and buggy until 1917. Cleburne was a good farming community. There were six cotton gins that ran constantly during the picking season. I remember much more rain in those days than now which let the farmers grow grain and feed as well as cotton.

My home address was 702 Featherstone Street. The large ornate wooden house was torn down and moved to a location near Grapevine, Texas, when my mother moved from

Cleburne about 1928. At the corner of Featherstone and Sunset Streets is an Adventist Church. This church was built about 1911. To commemorate the dedication of the church, the annual Adventist camp meeting was held in the vacant area across the street from our home. The men ran a water line from our front yard hydrant well down within the meeting grounds so that there would be water for the animals and the people in tents and covered wagons.

Before the camp meeting days, grain had been grown in a field there. Visualize a steam traction engine and a wheat thresher with grain hauling wagons with men in action.

At another time, there was a three-ring standard circus on this area. The cook tent was always set up first to feed the circus people. The big tent was in position, and here came the some 16 or so elephants to the circus location. They had been unloaded from their train cars downtown. The procession was ambling along with a half-asleep manhoot riding on the head of each elephant. A milk cow had been staked out to graze just off the street where the elephants were passing by. The cow bellowed and pawed the dust. The front elephant trumpeted and the action and yelling started. The elephants as a group did a right-face toward the cow as the manhoots slid off their heads and started beating the elephant trunks with their sticks. The front elephant gave another grunt; the procession turned and continued to the tent with the men walking.

Just west of where the Adventist Church now is (before the church was built our house was the last house on the street) there was the gate to the milk cow pasture. The boys brought the family milk cows for pasture during the daytime. The pasture was large, extending about to the county road south of the elementary school and up the hill west of McAnear Creek. (The school is very recent, but the road was roughed out then). The boys often hiked down in the pasture. Three of us were down there and we heard an airplane. Here

it comes. It was a biplane with the pilot sitting in the open. He
landed nearby in the cow pasture. We ran over to see the
airplane. He had run out of gas. "Will you boys keep the milk
cows off my plane while I go get some gas?" We would.
When he returned, he gave directions to help him get up
again. We held the end of the wings back until he got the
engine revved up; then we stepped back and up he went. For
watching the plane, he gave us a nickel. We went to the
nearest grocery store and got a nickel's worth of peppermint
stich candy at 20 cents a pound. We divided and each got 3
1/3 sticks.

In those days, McAnear Creek had running water with
edible size fish. If one stands on the elementary school yard
and looks south at the creek, he can see a high white rock
bluff. That is Rocky Bend. The water there was over-my-head;
I learned to swim in Rocky Bend.

For a number of years, Cleburne had street cars. The
line out our way came west from the courthouse on
Henderson Street. One line went north, and the other went
south on Douglas Avenue The south line went to
Featherstone Street, made a jog, and then went on south
some 2 or 3 miles to Love Lady Park. The park was at the
point where McAanear Creek, and east Buffalo and west
Buffalo creeks came together. It was a nice big park. Along
about 1906, or so, there was a Confederate Veteran Reunion
in Cleburne. Those old guys set up their tents as in combat
area; they stacked arms and followed bugle calls and other
camp activity. There were a number of old negros, probably
former slaves who did the cooking and other labor. We, white
boys were taught to call these old men, "Uncle". On one
occasion a man says, "Uncle, if you pray to the Lord to send
you a chicken, will He send you a chicken?! "Sir, Ise don't
know about that; if I pray to the Lord to send me out after a
chicken, I'll have chicken." There was a sham battle between

the veterans and the State militia. Lots of Bang-Bang with the veterans winning easily.

My mother belonged to an organization called The Daughters of the Confederacy. It was this group that arranged and set up the Confederate Monument on the Cleburne Courthouse Square. It was erected to be in place when the reunion was held. Look closely at this monument. The top is a four-sided cap. There was supposed to be a stature of a confederate soldier on top (The monument in Hillsboro has such a statue) Cleburne women couldn't get together the $300.00 necessary to purchase the statue of the Confederate Soldier. They did get together the $60 that the cap, cost.

Look at the comer stone of the Carnegie Library. It was built in Cleburne about the time I became interested in reading. Miss Rebecca Royal was the librarian. She took an interest in me and I had a supervised reading program for a number of years, Miss Royal came to Austin where she was Librarian for the Texas Supreme Court. The Carnegie Library has an auditorium upstairs. Many plays and other activities were put on there. (Notice how small it is).

Forest Avenue was the first paved street in Cleburne. In those days concrete was usually mixed in a wheelbarrow by hand. A man named Davenport had an engine driven concrete mixer. He and his men mixed and poured several square yards of paving a day. Four blocks were finally paved. Then the paving had to "cure" 21 days before traffic was permitted on it. Finally, the street was open to traffic with the speed limit at 12 miles per hour. In droves, people came over to "test their cars", and when they ran off the end of the paving, the police were there to arrest them for speeding. It was laughingly pointed out that traffic fines were going to pay for the paving.

It was before the paved street that I had my first auto ride. Mrs. Streetman, the Dentist's wife was an energetic individual. She could crank the side-cranked engine, she could shift gears, and she could guide with the tiller. One day she came puffinry along and recognized Mr. Cyrus' little boy. She stopped (I already was standing there with my mouth open) and asked if I would like to ride. I would. Behind the seat in the open-air car was a square box with a lid. I sat on this box for three or four blocks to where she turned off. Then I ran the remainder of the way home yelling, "I rode on an automobile."

Cleburne had a baseball team. The ballpark was several blocks south of the wagon yard which would make it some eight blocks southwest of the courthouse. There was a high board fence south on the north and east sides of the field; the west and west sides were open to the pasture and the mesquite trees. There was a shaded area of bleachers, and some not shaded. I didn't go to games because I didn't have the admission price. I did pay my 50¢ and go to a game when the Chicago White Sox on tour came to Cleburne. The score was 8 to 2 in favor of the Sox. Citizen reaction was--- That's a great score; our team was able to stand up like that with the Sox.

On one occasion, there was an airplane exhibit in the ballpark. Visitors to the exhibit sat on the regular seats; the plane flew in and landed and then took off again several times for the show. We boys didn't have the admission price and got over on the outfield in the mesquite trees. We eased up into the outfield, but the guards ran us back. (We could easily outrun the guards.) As the show went on, the guards got up closer to home plate to closer see the plane when it was on the ground. We boys climbed up into the tree nearest the outfield. (If the guards came toward us we could out run then.) The plane took off again. It headed toward our tree; the wheels touched the top branches of our tree. We had been closer to the airplane than the paying visitors, but that was too close. We climbed down and left.

I remember when the Post Office was built. My sister sang with the school group from the west steps at the dedication. There was a high brick fence east of the post office. On the east side of that fence an airplane was being constructed. One could see the activity from the sidewalk. There was a delay in completion until a propeller could be purchased. It cost $300. The propeller arrived; it was installed; it was revved up. A monkey wrench had been left on top wing. The wrench slid into propeller--Last of plane.

Sincerely yours,
Charles Cyrus

The Most Exciting Day of My Life
By Vivian Childers Cyrus
Written about 1987

I will never forget the day I boarded the train in Tipton Oklahoma to go to school in Belton Texas. Finishing high school in Tipton was not very exciting because my heart was in San Antonio where my class was graduating. The class of 1922 of Breckenridge High School where Edward Hertzberg and William Bradshaw were graduating 1st and 2nd at the top of the class of 300. Aunt Leila sent the newspaper clippings with pictures of two. She knew how much they meant to me. For the first two years of high school, Edward, William and I had had the same classes and the same program except for P.E., of course. We had a friendly rivalry about grades that kept me on my toes with homework and attendance

Now at last I was going to college like everyone in my class of sixteen in Tipton. Up to the middle of July we thought that Jennie – was going to Baylor with me and that would have been more fun for us both. That did not work out. Jennie went to her won church school. My family worked out the timetable for my leaving and for my arrival at Belton. This did not allow for the train from Tipton being late in Wichita Falls enough to miss connection with the train to Fort Worth.

I sat in the waiting room of that big station in Wichita Falls about 3PM wondering what I should do. The next train to Fort Worth would leave at 3AM the next morning. Somehow it didn't seem the right thing to try to stay awake and board that train in the wee hours of the morning. To your generation that would have been no problem. My parents had told me that the people at the information desk would be helpful if there was a problem. They were right. The Woman at the desk suggested that I turn in my ticket and purchase a pullman ticket. With that in hand, I could board the pullman car at 9:00, go to bed and the train would hook on to the pullman car at 3AM and I would be in Fort Worth to meet my Aunt Annie Glass, the next morning a 7:30. Whether I called my aunt or sent here a telegram I don't remember. We did not use telephones so easily as we do today. Cousin Lucille who was to meet me in Temple did not make it. In Temple we transferred to a train in Belton just eight miles away. The station was right on the campus. Since there were many girls doing the same thing it was not a scary transfer.

With all those transfers I made it fine but my trunk with all my possessions didn't. It was a week before that was on the loading dock at the depot. I had to pay $1.50 for a transfer man to deliver it to my dorm just two blocks away. This was an exciting time in my life. I realized I was on my own to pay for my board and room and my tuition with my own check book. The excitement was over when wrote the first check. It seemed so horrendous – so large that I feared my poor family wouldn't have enough left to buy groceries.

The last letter from Daddy was a dear one to me and I kept it for years[2]. He said he had been watching the checks in the bank and knew that I had only written the large one. By this time (it was October then) I must be needing some money to spend. In the envelope he enclosed a $5.00 bill. Take it and spend it on a party in your room. I was so thrilled and so were my three roommates. After buying another textbook for an Education course. I spent the rest on goodies and we had a party after lights were out at 10:00. I bet you can't figure out how we did it?

---

[2] Vivian's father Luther died a month later when his car was struck by a train.

My Family Background
By Vivian Childers Cyrus
[written about 1987]

Author's Note: *Below was Vivian's remembrances of her family history. There are many details that I cannot verify with other sources, but since she heard these stories directly from her older relatives, I think it is worth including them.*

Great Grandfather Louis Capt came to Texas from New York. He was born in Geneva Switzerland and went to school at The University of Paris. During his junior year he went with an Engineering Professor on a field trip to western Africa. There the party had bad luck and the natives turned against them. They were prisoners (the last three) and would have been killed had not one of them showed the natives how to skip rocks on the surface of the water. The natives considered them from the gods with this accomplishment and saved them. They flagged a ship bound for the United States. Louis was helpful in the boiler room and was soon given a job on board. He was employed on several trips between the United States and England. When he finished a trip in New York he decided to see what was out West. I don't know how he got to Texas. He was a resident of Austin, Texas in [blank]. He and his wife Elizabeth from Indiana had three sons while living in Austin where he had a wheelwright shop and blacksmith shop on Pecan St. Arnold Capt, the third child, was one year old when the family moved to the area of Dripping Springs. Arnold, our Grandfather, went to school at the Old Johnson Institute. The building still exists and is now used for Summer Camp by the Kidd family. Louis and Elizabeth had three other children.

     Louis Capt served his community by building grist mills on the creeks around Austin. He was continually having to replace them because they were washed away by heavy rains. It also was not a very lucrative occupation. The farmers brought their corn to be ground into meal or grit. For payment he received a portion. He built a house on Banco River just south of the town of Blanco. It is still standing and is in good condition I am told the hardwood floors were beautiful with square nails used.

My mother says she remembers Grandpa Capt sitting on his porch looking over the Blanco River. She went by many times of the day bringing water from the spring just below his house. That was their water supply.

Arnold Capt married Mary Talley of Dripping Springs and they came to live in Blanco. They had six children. My mother May was the third child. Leila Silliman was the first, Albert who moved to Arizona was the second, Earle was the fourth with Emmett and Bessie the fifth and sixth. They all had some college education after graduating from Blanco High School. Leila taught in San Antonio schools for thirty-five years. She earned a BS in Education from Baylor College in 1927.

May Capt married Luther M. Childers in August of 1904. It was a big wedding for Blanco Baptist Church. They went immediately to San Antonio where they lived for eleven years. Luther had a good job in a furniture store that was on Commerce St. in the same block of Joskes. He then moved the family to Elmer, Oklahoma where he had more opportunities in Banking.

Luther Childers came from Tippah County Mississippi. He was born the fourth child of Stephen and Linny Childers. Stephen was a successful farmer who had an interest in a sawmill and a cotton gin about nine miles from Riply, Mississippi. Stephen enlisted in the Confederate Army in Virginia. To be exact he and a friend fought in the cavalry. After the war was over, he and his friend walked home barefoot. He told Ethel, a cousin, that the friend was a slave.

Interview and/or Writing Prompts

My hope in compiling this family narrative is to help us save family stories that can't be revealed through simple vital records, like birth, marriage and death certificates. You can help save these stories by recording your own stories, or the stories of relatives.

There are a vast number of books and online resources available to give you good questions. This is intended to give you somewhere to start. Pick the questions that interest you. How you save the answers is up to you – audio recording, video recording or written down. Once you have a record, contact me and we'll talk about how we can save the record (bookmayer@me.com).

1. What is the earliest home you remember? Was it an apartment, house, farm, or… ? Who lived with you?

2. What do remember about daily life as a child? Did you have chores? (Favorite? Least favorite?)

3. In the summer, when you weren't in school, what was a day like for you? What was a day like during the school year?

4. How did you feel about school? Did you have a favorite teacher, coach or subject?

5. Did you have siblings? Tell us about your brothers and your sisters. What were your relationships like? Which sibling would you say you were closest to?

6. Did you have hobbies/activities/sports you liked to play as a kid?

7. Do you remember any particular road trip or vacation you took as a child?

8 What was your biggest challenge as a child?

9.What did you think you would do when you grow up?

10. Looking back, what do you think was wonderful about your childhood and what do you wish had been different?

11. Did you have a favorite relative or neighbor?

12. Did you family go to church or have any faith tradition? How did you feel about it?

13. How would you describe your mother (or father)? Did he/she work outside the home?

14. Did your mom or dad have favorite pastimes (cards, gardening, handiwork, bowling, etc.)?

15. Do you have any particularly good or funny memories of your mom or your dad?

16. What did your parents teach you that helped you later in life?

17. What was your first "real" job? What was your worst job? Did you have a favorite job?

18. Did any family members serve in the military? What stories did you hear about their service?

19. Did you know your grandparents? Tell about a time you spent with them.

20. Did you ever hear any stories about your great grandparents? What did you hear?

21. Did your family strongly identify with traditions from another country? If so, describe them.

22. What are you most proud of in your life?

23. What would you like your great grandkids in the future to know about you?

Feel free to contact me if you have any questions.
I would love to hear your stories! Feel free to email me or tell me about your experience on my Facebook page.

For more information and tips on saving family stories check:
www.familymemoriesmatter.com

www.facebook.com/memoriesmatterinterviews

Endnotes

[i] *Find A Grave.* Database with images.
https://www.findagrave.com/memorial/76709323: accessed 2019.
[ii] Swiss genealogy records are not widely digitized or translated at the time of this writing. Further documentation may require hiring a genealogist who specializes in Swiss records.
[iii] "Louis Capt," Obituary; photocopy of newspaper clipping, supplied October 8, 1991 by Clarice Cyrus Cowart in a letter to Carol and Glen Zumwalt. Personal property of Carla Mayer, Wheaton, IL.
[iv] [Ponca Indians Meeting], photograph, Date Unknown; (https://texashistory.unt.edu/ark:/67531/metapth38506/m1/1/?q=imag e%20indians: accessed June 11, 2019),University of North Texas Libraries, The Portal to Texas History, https://texashistory.unt.edu; crediting University of Texas at Arlington Library.
[v] Wilbarger, J.W., *Indian Depredations in Texas: Battles, Wars, Adventures, Forays, Murders, Massacres, etc. etc. Together with Biographical Sketches of Many of the Most Noted Indian Fighters and Frontiersmen of Texas.* First published by Hutchings Printing House, 1890. This edition printed 2019; 240-241.
[vi] Texas. "The Texas General Land Office" Database with images.(http://www.glo.texas.gov/ncu/SCANDOCS/archives_webfiles/ arcmaps/webfiles/landgrants/PDFs/2/9/4/294311.pdf: accessed 2019) Louis Capt, file no. 086.
[vii] See note vi.
[viii] Moursund, John Stribling, and Mabel Stribling. *Blanco County families for 100 years.* (Burnet, Texas: Nortex Press, c1981), p. 47.
[ix] See note iii.
[x] Duval, Johns C. *The Adventures of Big Foot Wallace.* Original edition printed by Claxton, Remsen, and Haffelfinger, Macon, GA 1871. Reprinted in 1983 by Time Life Books.
[xi] "Mrs. Mary L West Celebrates 82nd Birthday Monday," photocopy of newspaper article, *The Granger News,* exact date unknown. Personal property of Carla Mayer, Wheaton, IL.
[xii] *Presentation of First Historical Medallion In Blanco County.* Event Program. Blanco, Texas. March 16, 1963. Photocopy supplied by Jere Cyrus Smith.

xiii Osborn, William S. *Handbook of Texas Online*. http://www.tshaonline.org/handbook/online/articles/kbj09. Online article "JOHNSON INSTITUTE," accessed July 01, 2019.

xiv Cyrus, Vivian (Childers), Austin, Texas. Interview by Shirley Cyrus Mayer, 1980. Audio recording. Privately held by Carla Whitacre Mayer. Wheaton, Illinois; 2019.

xv Hunter, J Marvin. *The Trail Drivers of Texas*. "The Early Cattle Days in Texas." 1985, pp 362-366.

xvi "In Memory of Mary T. Capt" photocopied newspaper clipping, unsourced.

xvii 1900 U.S. Census, Blanco Texas, Justice Precinct 4, Ennumeration District 0008; image, Ancestry.com (http://www.ancestry.com: accessed July 2019; citing FHL microfilm 1241612.)

xviii First Baptist Church (Blanco, Texas), Marriage Certificate. Photocopy privately held by Carla Whitacre Mayer, Wheaton, IL.

xix See note xv.

xx War of 1812 Pension Application Files Index, 1812 -1815, Ancestry.com; accessed by Carla Mayer September 2019; Land warrant # Wt 41887 80 50 and # 28441 80 55

xxi According to Billy Owen's wife, Renelda Owen, Tommy Stanford was one hundred years old when Billy interviewed him. The interview took place around 1976. (Email from Renelda Owen to Carla Whitacre Mayer, dated September 24, 2019, privately held by Carla Whitacre Mayer, Wheaton, IL)

xxii Covington, Tommy. *The History of Tippah County Mississippi* (Tippah, Mississippi, The Society 1981)

xxiii Confederate Pension Application, State of Mississippi, "Anna Childers Declaration" September 10,1864, photocopy of original, privately held by Carla Whitacre Mayer, Wheaton, IL.

xxiv 1900 U.S. Census, Beat 4, Tippah, Mississippi; Page 8 ; Enumeration District 0109; FHL microfilm: 1240829.

xxv See note xxii

xxvi Cyrus, Vivian Childers. "Memory Book." MS. Dickinson, Texas, 1987. Privately held by Carla Whitacre Mayer, Wheaton, IL, 2019.

xxvii Oklahoma. Oklahoma State Board of Health. Death Certificate no 71256, Luther Molver Childers (1922). Bureau of Vital Statistics, Oklahoma City.

xxviii Photo privately held by Renelda Owen, Oxford, MS 2018. It came from the house of Esker and Mazie Childers and was labeled "OK house"

xxix Childers, William (Frederick, OK) to"Dear Escar" [Eskar Childers]. Letter. 27 April 1927. Privately held by Renelda Owen, Oxford, MS 2019.

xxx1930; U.S. Census: San Antonio, Bexar, Texas; Page: 19B; Enumeration District: 0118; FHL microfilm: 2342031

xxxi Childers, Mae Capt (San Antonio, TX) to "Dear Mazie" [Mazie Latham Childers]. Letter. 16 August 1951. Privately held by Renelda Owen, Oxford, MS 2019.

xxxii Ball, Doris LeClerc. *The Ball Families of the Potomac* (Stevenson's Genealogy Center, 2004)

xxxiii 1880; Census Place: Louisville, Winston, Mississippi; Roll: 669; Family History Film: 1254669; Page: 1B; Enumeration District: 021; Image: 0197

xxxiv Rea, R. N., "A Mississippi Soldier of the Confederacy", in *The Confederate Veteran 1922 Volume 30* (Nashville: S.A. Cunningham). 262.

xxxv McLean, Jess N. *The Official Records of the 13th Mississippi Infantry Regiment of Volunteers* (Create Space, 2017).

xxxvi Compiled Service Record, John L. Ball, Pvt. Co. B 13 Mississippi Infantry. Accessed on Fold3.com September 2019 by Carla Whitacre Mayer, Wheaton, IL.

xxxvii Ball, Empriss Jowell. "The History of Dr. John Lewis Ball Family: Beginning September 15, 1840" May 1967. Unpublished. Privately held by Carla Whitacre Mayer, Wheaton, IL.

xxxviii Baylor Women's College (now Baylor University). College Transcripts for Jennie Lewis Ball,1890.

xxxix Kentucky. Logan County. Court Records for Henry Cyrus. 20 may, 1811: Order Book 5 p 144 Logan County KY

xl Paddock, B.B. *A Twentieth Century History of West and North Texas* (Ann Arbor, MI Lewis Publishing Company, 1970)

xli Cyrus, Addie Scales (Doll), "What I Know and Remember About My Father Charles Lewis Cyrus", date unknown. Privately held by Carla Mayer, Wheaton IL. 2019

xlii Cyrus, Charles (Dickinson, TX) to "Dear Ann" [Ann Murphy]. Letter. 18 September 1983. Privately held by Carla Whitacre Mayer, Wheaton, IL.

xliii Cyrus, Charles. Austin, Texas. Interview by Shirley Cyrus Mayer, 1980. Audio recording. Privately held by Carla Whitacre Mayer. Wheaton, Illinois; 2019.

xliv Cyrus, Addie Scales (Doll), "What I Know and Remember About My Father Charles Lewis Cyrus", date unknown. Privately held by Carla Mayer, Wheaton IL. 2019

xlv Cyrus, Charles (Dickinson, TX) to "Dear Ann" [Ann Murphy]. Letter. March 1984. Privately held by Carla Whitacre Mayer, Wheaton, IL.

xlvi Addie Pinck Scales is also a direct descendant to Valentine Allen.